PROJECT BASED LEARNING
TOOLKIT SERIES

PBL
STARTER KIT

*To-the-Point Advice, Tools and Tips for
Your First Project in Middle or High School*

BUCK INSTITUTE
FOR EDUCATION

**PROJECT BASED LEARNING
FOR THE 21ST CENTURY**

About the Buck Institute for Education

The Buck Institute for Education (BIE) is dedicated to improving 21st century teaching and learning by creating and disseminating products, practices, and knowledge for effective Project Based Learning. Founded in 1987, BIE is a not-for-profit 501(c)3 organization that receives operational funding from the Leonard and Beryl Buck Trust, and funding from other education organizations, foundations, schools and school districts, state educational agencies and national governments for product development, professional development, and research.

PBL STARTER KIT

Principal Author
John Larmer

Secondary Authors
David Ross
John R. Mergendoller, PhD

Published by Buck Institute for Education
18 Commercial Boulevard., Novato, California 94949 USA
www.bie.org

June 2009: First Edition.

Printed by Unicorn Printing Specialists, San Rafael, California.
Printed on acid-free paper with soy-based ink.
Designed by Pam Scrutton, San Francisco, California.

ISBN 978-0-9740343-2-4

PROJECT BASED LEARNING
TOOLKIT SERIES

PBL STARTER KIT

Table of Contents

TABLE OF CONTENTS

Foreword: About BIE's *PBL Toolkit Series*

You hold in your hands all you need to start your first project—except, of course, your own idea for what it should be about. This book will guide you in finding that idea, then making it work in your classroom with careful planning and skillful execution. The *PBL Starter Kit* is designed for teachers in middle and high schools; a version of this book for K-5 teachers, *PBL in the Elementary Grades*, is also published by BIE.

BIE is publishing the *PBL Toolkit Series* to help teachers and schools do PBL more effectively. Because if it's not done right, or it's done for the wrong reasons ("someone told us to do it"), PBL will either be a waste of time or, worse yet, backfire on a teacher unprepared for its challenges. PBL is not just one more instructional strategy to try. PBL, done well, requires substantial changes in how teachers teach and how schools are organized. The *PBL Starter Kit* is the first in a series of short books on specific topics related to Project Based Learning. Some titles are for more experienced PBL practitioners, some are for school leaders, and some are for teachers of particular subjects or students.

Each *Toolkit* is built around a combination of examples, guidance, and resources. More information and help, including research, professional development and coaching, project libraries and videos, and the acclaimed *PBL Handbook,* can be found at the BIE website, **www.bie.org**. An online PBL training program co-created by BIE is available at **pbl-online.org**. And you can watch short videos of students and teachers planning and doing PBL on BIE's YouTube channel, YouTube/BIEPBL.

Good luck! Send us your comments about the *PBL Starter Kit* and other BIE resources so we can make them better. Please email your thoughts—and success stories too—to feedback@bie.org.

John R. Mergendoller, Ph.D.
Executive Director

Acknowledgements

Like other authors, we stand on the shoulders of those who have taught us — in this case, about what it means to do effective PBL. Many individuals contributed to this book through example and idea, and it is impossible to acknowledge them all. Some specific individuals, however, have given of their time and wisdom, and we wish to express our gratitude and appreciation.

The following teachers contributed the Spotlight Projects that are highlighted as examples throughout the book: Kristine Kurpiewski, ASPIRA Early College High School, Chicago; Anne Gloag, High Tech High School, San Diego; Jennifer Ransier, Patrick F. Taylor Science and Technology Academy, New Orleans; Kristin Russo and Paul Koh, City Arts and Technology High School, San Francisco; Donita Massing, Miami Valley Career and Technical Center, Dayton, Ohio.

David Ross, BIE Director of Professional Development, developed initial ideas for the book, wrote pieces of it, and contributed many valuable insights plus one of his projects to "Spotlight" from his teaching days at Napa New Technology High School.

The development of rubrics for 21st century skills found in this book was capably spearheaded by Juliane Blazevski, Ph.D., Executive Director of Hypothesi, LLC. Pam Scrutton has done an outstanding job making the book's message more understandable through her design. Our cover photo of students at Mare Island Technical Academy in Vallejo, CA was taken by Anne Dowie, and we thank them all.

As with all BIE products, this book was reviewed by a number of educators. These included the teachers who contributed Spotlight Projects as well as Jane Douglass and Ashley Carruth of Basalt Middle School, Basalt CO; Katie Wade of Redwood High School, Larkspur CA; David Siegfried, Teacher-in-Residence at the Coalition of Essential Schools; and Tara Donoghue of Tamalpais HS, Mill Valley CA. This book is better as a result of your critiques, and we thank you.

John Larmer, BIE's Director of Product Development, was the principal author of this book and is the editor of the *PBL Toolkit Series*. We are grateful for his hard work and appreciative of his turns of phrase.

Buck Institute for Education
Novato, CA
June 2009

INTRODUCTION

You've heard about Project Based Learning, but now you're wondering... Sure, it sounds good, but is it right for me and my students? Isn't it a big change? Can I do it in today's educational landscape? Our answer is yes, yes, and yes — with some "buts and ifs" we'll explore in this book. By the end, we hope you'll be planning to conduct your first project.

The Purpose of This Book

This book is written for teachers who are new to Project Based Learning, which we'll refer to as PBL from now on. The *PBL Starter Kit* is designed to provide easy to read, brief and to-the-point advice about your first project, and some tools to help you do it well. Other books in the BIE *PBL Toolkit Series* are meant to include the veterans — this one is for the rookies.

Specifically, this book is written for teachers who:

- **Teach in a high school or middle school**, although the basic design of PBL we describe can work for any grade level.

- **Teach in any subject area**, although our examples are drawn mainly from typical core academic courses.

- **Are considering using PBL**, but have not been to PBL workshops or read books on PBL methodology.

- **May have tried "doing projects" but were unsatisfied**, and would like to try it again, differently.

How This Book is Organized

The *PBL Starter Kit* has eight chapters:

I. The **Introduction** provides background information about PBL and explains what teaching is like in a project based classroom.

II. **Spotlight Projects** describes six sample projects from various schools, subject areas, and grade levels. We draw examples from these projects throughout the rest of the book.

III. **Getting Started** takes you through the process of developing ideas for your project, setting goals for student learning, deciding on the project's scope, and writing a Driving Question.

IV. **Planning and Preparing** gets down to the nitty-gritty details: how to design the tasks and products students will complete, assess their work, launch the project, form groups, provide resources and lessons, create a schedule, and make logistical arrangements.

V. **Managing Your Project** shows you what to do once a project is underway: how to build the right classroom culture, guide the process of inquiry, manage day-to-day tasks, stay organized, facilitate student presentations to an audience, and troubleshoot problems.

VI. **Reflect and Perfect** explains how, after your project, you and your students should reflect on the results, note ideas for improvement, and celebrate a job well done.

VII. **After the Last Bell: Closing Thoughts** raises some questions to consider before doing another project, and concludes with comments from Spotlight Project teachers.

VIII. **Useful Stuff** contains project planning forms, sample rubrics, and student handouts.

As you are reading, you will see the following special features:

TIPS FROM THE CLASSROOM

Advice on various topics from experienced PBL teachers.

Additional examples, resources, or notes on specific topics.

*USE THIS

Reminder that a form or handout can be found in **Useful Stuff**, the back section of the book.

How to Use This Book

This book is meant to be used to actually plan a project while you read it. We provide copy masters of the following three planning forms in the Useful Stuff section, or you can use the online versions available at **www.bie.org**.

- **Project Overview** — A two-page form for recording a summary of your project

- **Project Teaching and Learning Guide** — A one-page form to record your plans for helping students learn what they need to be successful in the project

- **Project Calendar** — A one-page form for recording the daily use of time in your project

Although it's not absolutely vital, we encourage you to fill out these forms as you go through each chapter — we'll remind you. You'll also see examples of completed forms from our Spotlight Projects.

> This book is meant to be used to actually plan a project while you read it.

What is Project Based Learning?

Do you ever feel like you're pushing your students through the course you teach, or herding reluctant cattle with a combination of encouragement, rewards, and threats? In Project Based Learning, it's different. Students are *pulled* through the curriculum by a meaningful question to explore, an engaging real-world problem to solve, or a design challenge to meet. Before they can do this, they need to work with other students to inquire into the issues raised, learn content and skills, develop an answer or solution, create high-quality products, and then present their work to other people. This process creates a strong need to know and understand the material. And that's the key to increasing students' motivation to learn in PBL — give them a *real* need to know, understand, and demonstrate what they learn, beyond simply getting a good grade.

Essential Elements of PBL

Whatever form a project takes, it must have these essential elements to meet our definition of PBL:

- **Significant content**. At its core, the project is focused on teaching students important knowledge and skills, derived from standards and key concepts at the heart of academic content areas.

- **21st century skills**. Students build skills valuable for today's world, such as critical thinking/problem solving, collaboration, and communication, which are taught and assessed.

- **In-depth inquiry**. Students are engaged in a rigorous, extended process of asking questions, using resources, and developing answers.

- **Driving Question**. Project work is focused by an open-ended question that students explore or that captures the task they are completing.

- **Need to know**. Students see the need to gain knowledge, understand concepts, and apply skills in order to create project products, beginning with an Entry Event that generates interest and curiosity.

- **Voice and choice**. Students are allowed to make some choices about the products to be created, how they work, and how they use their time, guided by the teacher and depending on age level and PBL experience.

- **Revision and reflection**. The project includes processes for students to use feedback to consider additions and changes that lead to high-quality products, and think about what and how they are learning.

- **Public audience**. Students present their work to other people, beyond their classmates and teacher.

PBL Misconceptions

PBL is not: *the dessert*

PBL is: *the main course*

A project is central to the curriculum and drives your instruction; it is not a "fun activity" or "applied learning" you let students do after a traditionally-taught unit. PBL is both a curriculum organizer and an instructional method.

PBL is not: *a string of activities tied together under a theme, concept, time period, culture, geographic area, etc.*

PBL is: *set of learning experiences and tasks that guide students in inquiry toward answering a central question, solving a problem, or meeting a challenge.*

For example, an interdisciplinary unit on the Renaissance in which students build a model of a machine based on a Da Vinci drawing, write and present a report on a famous artist, and perform a costumed drama about a historical event is not necessarily PBL. These activities *could* be part of a PBL unit if together they help students develop and present an answer to a central question such as "Was the Renaissance just a rebirth, or a whole new baby?" In this case, the unit was "activity based" but did not require rigorous inquiry into a central question.

PBL is not: *the same as "making something" or "hands-on learning" or "doing an activity."*

PBL is: *often focused on creating physical artifacts, but not always. It must involve other intellectually challenging tasks and products focused on research, reading, writing, discussion and oral presentation.*

It's not truly PBL if students are *simply* making a collage about a novel, constructing a model of the pyramids, analyzing water samples from a lake, or measuring and calculating the geometry of buildings. These artifacts and activities *could* be part of a rigorous project if they help students meet a complex challenge and develop and present an answer to a central question.

PBL's Effectiveness: What Experience and Research Tells Us

Project Based Learning has had its advocates in education for many years, but more and more teachers and schools in the 21st century are recognizing its value.

Classroom teachers, based on their experience, say that a well-designed and well-implemented project:

- Can work for all kinds of students, with the right support

- Improves students' motivation to learn

- Can be used to teach academic content standards

- Can include multiple opportunities to integrate technology

- Helps students see how school connects to the outside world by making learning relevant and meaningful

- Promotes greater civic participation and global awareness

Researchers have found that well-designed and well-implemented PBL can:

- Be *more* effective than traditional instruction in increasing academic achievement

- Increase student motivation and engagement in learning

- Improve students' retention of knowledge over time

- Improve students' mastery of 21st century skills

- Be especially effective with lower-achieving students

- Increase students' achievement on state-administered, standardized tests

Researchers also would say, naturally, that PBL needs more research, because it has been hard to pin down — so much depends on how it is defined, the particular circumstances in a school, and the quality of classroom implementation.

For more about the research on PBL, including links to specific studies and reprints of research articles, see the research section of the BIE website, **www. bie.org**.

Schools have used PBL effectively in all grade levels and courses, and for these special purposes:

- Career/technical education programs; continuation/alternative high school programs; after-school programs; summer school

- Integrating two or more school subjects and encouraging team teaching

- Connecting the school to other schools, the community, businesses, and other organizations

A school as whole can help make PBL effective by creating a supportive culture, encouraging collaboration among teachers, providing professional development, and developing school-wide practices and assessments. For more on this topic, check the BIE website, www.bie.org.

The Role of the Teacher in PBL

Once teachers feel comfortable with PBL, they usually say they'd "never go back." They see how well it works for their students, and they enjoy the new role they play. PBL allows a teacher to work more closely with students, acting more like a coach instead of the "sage on the stage."

> Once teachers feel comfortable with PBL, they usually say they'd "never go back."

Now, if you *enjoy* being the center of attention in your classroom, you may think PBL is not for you. But don't fret—there are times when you still will be the focus. Because you know more about the subject, you might still give a lecture, provide a structured lesson, or direct students to resources. Especially in your early projects, you'll still be planning and facilitating much of the work. In future projects as your students are more able to work independently, you may need to plan and facilitate less and less, but you still play a vital role as manager of the inquiry process, assessor of learning, and master of logistics. And if teaching a la PBL feels challenging at first, be assured that your skills will improve over time, as you learn from each project.

We'll say more about your role in the chapters that follow, as it relates to specific steps along the way toward planning and managing a successful project. But first, kick back and let's see what PBL actually looks like in real classrooms.

 **Bulletin Board**

PBL Prepares Students for 21st Century Challenges

"Let's be clear — we are failing too many of our children. We're sending them out into a 21st century economy by sending them through the doors of 20th century schools."

> — Barack Obama, in a speech at the Center for American Progress

Lots of people are saying the same thing: teaching and learning have to be different in today's world. Education leaders, business leaders, academics and the authors below sound a similar note:

"Countries like India are now able to compete for global knowledge work as never before — and America had better get ready for this."

> — Thomas Friedman, *The World Is Flat*

"Nations around the world are reforming their school systems… to support the more complex knowledge and skills needed in the 21st century, skills needed for framing problems, seeking and organizing information and resources, and working strategically with others to manage and address dilemmas and create new products."

> — Linda Darling-Hammond, *Powerful Learning*

"Current formal education still prepares students primarily for the world of the past, rather than for possible worlds of the future."

> — Howard Gardner, *Five Minds for the Future*

"There is a profound disconnect between what students are taught and tested on in most high schools today and how they are expected to learn, versus what the world will demand of them as adults and what motivates them to do their best."

> — Tony Wagner, *The Global Achievement Gap*

SPOTLIGHT PROJECTS

We've chosen six projects to help provide you with a clear idea of what it means to design and implement a project. These projects are from different teachers and schools, different subject areas, and illustrate the different forms PBL can take even when the projects are relatively limited in scope:

- 9th grade Introductory Science: "Product Comparison"

- 10th-11th grade Algebra II/Trigonometry: "Projectile Motion"

- 11-12th grade English and U.S. Government: "Banned in America"

- 7th grade Life Science: "A Balancing Act"

- 11th grade U.S. History: "American Archetypes"

- 11th-12th grade Information Technology/Business/Arts: "Design and Attract"

The teachers you're about to meet were not veteran PBL practitioners when they launched these projects. So you might notice some weak spots or things you might change, or have ideas about how to expand the project. We'll be discussing some of the details of these projects in the chapters to come, and you can find more information about them on the websites noted.

Project #1: Product Comparison
(9th grade Science)

THE PROJECT IN BRIEF

Project Title: Product Comparison

Project Author: Kristine Kurpiewski, ASPIRA Early College Middle School, Chicago

Subject Area: Introductory Science

Grade Level: 9th

Duration: 12 hours of class time

Driving Question: Which consumer products are most reliable?

Project Summary: Students function as a research team determining the most reliable brand of a product — that is, the one that best does what it is supposed to do. The teams choose a product commonly found at a supermarket and determine which of its qualities are most important for consumers. These qualities must be testable. The teams choose three examples of the selected product, create a hypothesis, then design and perform an experiment to test it. The teams exchange products and experimental protocols with another group, embark on a second round of testing to compare results, and discuss their conclusions in a PowerPoint presentation given to an audience.

Major Student Products: Research summary with data table; written report of testing protocols and hypothesis; oral presentation and defense of test results and interpretation.

For More Information: This project has not yet been posted to a website; email info@bie.org for contact information.

How the Project Was Conceived and Planned

Kristine Kurpiewski teaches Introductory Science in urban Chicago at the ASPIRA Early College High School, and knows her adolescent students well. They are a diverse mix of 9th graders who often need their skills built from the ground up. They are more motivated by classroom work that reflects their everyday experience than they are by textbooks and worksheets. And since sitting still for long periods of time can be a challenge, they enjoy being active learners. So Kristine turned to Project Based Learning. She wanted to design a project to introduce her students to the scientific method at the beginning of her course.

> Driving Question: Which consumer products are most reliable?

The seed of her project came from a familiar resource — a textbook she had used for years in middle school. Buried in the inter-chapter pages of the teacher's guide was a suggestion for a weeklong series of labs that focus on the scientific method, which Kristine had been slowly expanding over the years to increase their depth and breadth. She wanted a project that would tie the multiple lab experiences together. Her inspiration came during a visit to a local supermarket when she read the competing claims for quality and safety on the labels of several well-known products. What if she put students into groups that would function as independent product testing laboratories? She could then train her students to think and act like scientists while they examined familiar household goods.

With the project idea firmly in hand, Kristine turned to the Illinois Learning Standards. She found a cluster she wanted to focus on: conducting controlled experiments; collecting and organizing data; formulating alternative hypotheses; defending conclusions to an audience.

How the Project Was Managed

To begin, Kristine raised students' interest in the project by leading a discussion about whether we can always believe the claims made about various products we buy. She showed students some examples of product tests in *Consumer Reports* magazine. During the first week of the project Kristine trained her students how to develop and refine a hypothesis, design an experiment with controlled variables, and record data. Then students worked in groups of four to design testing protocols for a consumer product that could easily be found in local stores, such as paper towels, batteries, adhesive tape, diapers, and laundry detergents.

During the second week of the project each group ran multiple tests on its product. For example, the paper towel groups focused on water absorption and tensile strength, pouring various amounts of water on towels and pulling on them with increasing weight. Batteries were tested for how long they last, tape for its strength. One lucky group counted the number of chocolate chips in cookies. The testing procedure was designed and written up carefully so it could be replicated by other "scientists," just like it would be in the real world. Students then switched protocols and products with another group and enacted a second round of testing. During the project's final week, each group analyzed both sets of testing data and then created a PowerPoint presentation that was delivered to students and faculty, who functioned in two roles: concerned citizens and critical lab supervisors.

Reflecting on the Project

According to Kristine, the results of *Product Comparison* exceeded her expectations. The Driving Question was answered; students could say which products were best and support their conclusion with sound evidence. Her students were actively engaged, thinking hard, and mastering the scientific skills listed in the standards. They were learning how to work together as a group, manage their time and materials, and present to an audience. One of the unintended outcomes of Kristine's project turned out to be cross-curricular; students saw that they were applying skills in they had learned in math class to their science investigations. Her math teacher colleagues noted that students stopped asking why they needed to learn the metric system, because they knew from their lab work in Kristine's room that scientists use grams and millimeters, not ounces and inches.

Reflecting on the outcomes achieved, Kristine noted:

"My students did gain a lot. After this project they know exactly what to do during an experiment. I barely have to prompt them. They have a template for a lab experiment in their notebooks. When they have to do an experiment now, they say, "We know how to do this. We've done this before. We know how to write a hypothesis. We know how to design an experiment.

"At first I was concerned about spending three weeks on this project but when I look back I realize how much my students learned and how much time I save by not having to re-teach the same thing over and over again. I realize how important it was to take my time and do this right."

Project #2 : Projectile Motion
(10th-11th grade Math)

THE PROJECT IN BRIEF

Project Title: Projectile Motion

Project Author: Anne Gloag, High Tech High School, San Diego

Subject Area: Math (Algebra II/Trigonometry)

Grade Level: 10th-11th

Duration: 14 hours of class time

Driving Question: How can we build a device to launch a projectile and calculate its motion in order to hit a target?

Project Summary: Students work in groups to design and construct a ballistic device that launches an object in a flight path that follows a parabola. They use low cost materials (PVC pipe, plywood, rubber bands, etc.) to build the device, which must be capable of repeated firings. Students participate in multiple tests and use the data they record to redesign their device if needed. Each team makes an oral presentation using PowerPoint slides to summarize their findings.

Major Student Products: Design proposal, working model of a ballistic device, testing report, data analysis report, redesign report, PowerPoint and oral presentation.

For More Information: High Tech High: http://projects.hightechhigh.org/

How the Project Was Conceived and Planned

Anne Gloag's successful real-world background — a PhD in math, the founding of a small company, applied research in a complex field — didn't cloud her understanding of the teenage mind. When she became a math teacher at High Tech High School in urban San Diego she was prepared for the students she would lead. Loud noise and a small dose of destruction, she trusted, could go a long way toward engaging her students and meeting her academic goals.

> Driving Question: How can we build a device to launch a projectile and calculate its motion in order to hit a target?

The study of parabolas, Anne knew, offered fundamental mathematical concepts she wanted her Algebra II/ Trigonometry students to understand at the beginning of the semester. She had seen a related project run by her peers teaching physics, so she decided to borrow their idea and expand upon it. And so *Projectile Motion* was born as a challenge to her students: use math to design and construct a device that can launch an object to hit a target. She wondered, briefly, how some parents and administrators might react when they heard students were going to be firing ballistic missiles into the air, but she planned for safety and knew her students would not object — far from it. As Anne says, "Unfortunately, most of the parabolas in the real world are related to weapons systems. But it just made sense to use that fact of everyday life to shape my project."

Some of Anne's goals for her students came from California's content standards for Algebra II, Trigonometry, and Physics, including: "solving and graphing quadratic equations by factoring, completing the square, or using the quadratic formula"; "using trigonometry to determine unknown sides or angles in right triangles"; and "knowing how to solve two-dimensional trajectory problems." But Anne, along with her school, has additional goals that *Projectile Motion* allows her to reach. She wants her students to be strong collaborators, so they work in groups for this project. She wants them to be problem solvers, which they are when they analyze results from their test firings to redesign their device. Finally, she encourages creativity by giving students the opportunity to let their imaginations run free in the initial design phase of the project.

How the Project Was Managed

When Anne presented students with their challenge she gave them a few technical specifications for the device, such as the size of the projectile to be fired, the minimum distance it must travel, and the size of the target. The projectile (a small potato, actually) was to be propelled by either compressed air or tension-release, like a slingshot. Shortly after students were told of their challenge and understood that they needed to know mathematical concepts, Anne provided direct instruction to give them the necessary background knowledge for the tasks they would face. Then she cut them loose with blank pieces of paper and a few design guidelines to begin the brainstorming phase of design, sketching out ideas on paper amid lively discussions.

After the design phase students spent three days constructing their devices, using low-cost materials like plastic pipe, plywood, and rubber bands. Excitement built during the initial test firings. Students collected data from the test firings and took photos, which they used to write the first of a series of reports. That data was used to embark on major redesigns, which required a second round of testing and reports. The project concluded when each group created PowerPoint slides and made an oral presentation, to their peers and Anne, to explain their procedures, data and conclusions.

Reflecting on the Project

Anne was pleased with the results of *Projectile Motion*. Students learned the math well and improved their skills in several areas, like working in teams, problem-solving, and making presentations. Overall, students enjoyed a chance to make real the theorems, proofs and logarithms they encounter in advanced algebra and trigonometry. And for Anne, that's confirmation of her own experience using math in the real world.

Anne explained the value of the project:

"I make a point of bringing this complex material down to earth. I must make it relevant. When I do that, they learn more.

"The students really liked the hands-on aspect of the project. They connected the equations and mathematical methods they learned in the direct instruction component of the unit with a concrete application. I found that when I come back and talked about functions in the classroom I could refer back to this project in order to get students to think what x-intercepts mean and what the maximum and minimum points of a function mean."

Project #3: Banned in America!

(11th-12th grade English/Language Arts and U.S. Government)

THE PROJECT IN BRIEF

Project Title: Banned in America!

Project Authors: Kristin Russo and Paul Koh, City Arts and Technology High School, San Francisco

---

Subject Area: Language Arts (with U.S. Government)

Grade level: 11th and 12th

Duration: 20 hours of class time

Driving Question: Should censorship play a role in society?

Project Summary: Students read a book of their choosing from a list of books that have been banned at some time in the U.S., and discuss their books in peer reading groups. They write a persuasive essay, in the form of a letter, about whether or not their book should be banned at their school. To culminate the project, students stage a mock trial to dramatize issues of free speech and the role of censorship.

Major Student Products: Persuasive Essay (individual), participation in a mock trial (group).

For More Information: Envision Schools Project Exchange: **http://www.envisionprojects.org/cs/envision/view/env_p/78**

How the Project Was Conceived and Planned

There is probably no better way to enrage an English teacher than to start talking about banning books. Kristin Russo, who teaches Language Arts at City Arts and Technology (CAT) High School in San Francisco, is no exception. Over the years she frequently visited the American Library Association (ALA) website and one day she noticed that it devoted an entire section of the site to banned books. Since 1982, the ALA has been scheduling Banned Books Week for the last week of September in an attempt to draw national attention to the importance of the freedoms we often take for granted. This inspired Kristin to work with her teaching partner Paul Koh, who teaches U.S. Government, to develop a four-week project for 11th graders that examined the role of censorship in America. An earlier project in which CAT students developed their own definitions of the American Dream — which often involved freedom — helped set the context for the further examination of U.S. politics and society in *Banned in America!*

> Driving Question: Should censorship play a role in society?

The curriculum specialists at ALA offer a wide range of activities for teachers who wished to explore censorship. Kristin and Paul added a few goals of their own. Paul wanted his students to learn about the First Amendment. Kristin's goals included building reading and writing skills, as well as literary analysis skills as defined in California's English/Language Arts standards. The teaching team also wanted to encourage their students' collaborative work skills. To demonstrate achievement of these goals, students were asked to complete two major products: an individual persuasive essay (in the form of a letter) on whether a book should be banned, and participation in one of four staged trials concerning a censorship issue.

How the Project Was Managed

Kristin and Paul launched the project by raising students' awareness of the fact that certain books had been banned at times in some communities in the U.S. As an example, they read students *In the Night Kitchen* by Maurice Sendak and poems by Shel Silverstein. The class discussed the 1983 *Pico* Supreme Court case, in which a school board ordered books it characterized as "anti-American, anti-Christian, anti-Semitic, and just plain filthy" to be removed from high school and junior high school libraries. This got students somewhat riled up, then the teachers launched the project by presenting a hypothetical situation: How would you respond if our principal had on his desk a proposal to ban several books being used in your school?

Students were primed to jump right into project work. They received a list of banned books from the ALA website and picked one title to read. Some students chose the same book as some of their peers, but even students who read a book on their own were placed into peer reading and editing groups, much like literature circles. Students studied the constitutional issues of the *Pico* case and researched the censorship-related history of the book they were reading, which they had to include in their persuasive letter to the principal. They wrote multiple drafts of their individual essays while they prepared for the mock trials. Student engagement was in part driven by the knowledge that the mock trials would be held before a group of adult volunteers and visitors who would form a jury and decide the merits of the arguments they heard.

Reflecting on the Project

Kristin and Paul were pleased with the student work and thinking that emerged from the project. The teachers learned a lot too, as they had to develop strategies to monitor groups engaged in multiple activities simultaneously. The project produced some unforeseen challenges for Kristin. Despite her strong background in literature, she found herself struggling to assist groups who had chosen books she didn't know when they were turned loose to explore the broad reading list provided by the ALA.

Afterward, Kristin and Paul commented on their project's challenges and outcomes:

"The purpose of this unit was to combine the content from banned books and First Amendment rights in an engaging forum for students. When we were planning the difficulty we had was to authentically combine the content from both subject areas.

"Despite the ways in which this project could have been improved, we felt that it was a great way to execute a unit on banned books. Students read with intent, wrote persuasive essays, and used the knowledge attained in an exhibition. When the mock trials were completed, students were very proud of what they did, and many students who felt like their public speaking skills were lacking proved themselves in front of their peers."

Project #4: A Balancing Act

(7th grade Life Science)

THE PROJECT IN BRIEF

Project Title: A Balancing Act

Project Author: Jennifer Ransier, (formerly at) Jefferson Parish School of Science and Technology, New Orleans

Subject Area: Life Science

Grade level: 7th

Duration: 15 hours of class time

Driving Question: How can we design a completely self-sustaining ecosystem?

Project Summary: Students act as "set designers" for a TV reality show who need to propose a working ecosystem for an artificial biosphere. Each team is assigned a particular ecosystem: a rain forest, a desert, fresh water ponds and swamps, tundra, grasslands, coniferous forest, and a decid-uous forest. Students conduct research on their ecosystem as they learn about the characteristics of all ecosystems and build understanding of what makes a balanced ecosystem work. In preparation for an oral presentation of their proposals, student groups create detailed posters and a written report.

Major Student Products: Written report on a particular ecosystem; detailed poster showing "set design" of the ecosystem; oral presentation of set design proposal; second written report on a disturbance to the ecosystem.

For More Information: This project has not yet been posted to a website; email info@bie.org for contact information.

How the Project Was Conceived and Planned

Middle school teacher Jennifer Ransier wisely decided to capitalize on pop culture to capture the attention of her 7th grade life science students. Reality TV shows were everywhere, so Jennifer gave her students an opportunity to help design one—and, by the way, to learn some important science about ecosystems. The idea first occurred to her while searching the Internet for projects, where she ran across a college Biology class whose assignment was "create life." Jennifer adapted this task for her students by creating the context of a human-built biosphere where contestants on a reality show would live. The students' job as set consultants would be to propose a working ecosystem for the biosphere. With simplified requirements and adequate scaffolding, she knew her students would be up to the challenge.

> Driving Question: How can we design a completely self-sustaining ecosystem?

The goals for the *A Balancing Act* project included state of Louisiana Grade Level Expectations for 7th grade science, including the factors of ecology such as biotic and abiotic features, symbiosis, predator/prey relationships, animal adaptations, non-native species, and the effects of human interactions on ecosystems. In addition, students would need to learn how to find and use information from online and print sources; how to make an oral presentation; and how to use graphic design skills to create effective posters. Finally, Jennifer wanted her students to practice their collaboration skills and build their ability to organize project work, conduct research effectively, and manage time well.

To demonstrate achievement of these goals, Jennifer decided to have students create a detailed poster showing the proposed set design for their ecosystem, to be used in an oral presentation. A written report was also required. Both products needed to explain what consumers, producers, decomposers, and relationships would be needed to make an ecosystem survive without excessive competition or depletion.

How the Project Was Managed

A Balancing Act began when students received a "memo from Wolf Television," explaining their goals for the success of a new reality show, "Beat the Biosphere." The set design teams are asked to come up with proposals for a variety of functioning ecosystems, such as a rain forest, desert, fresh water ponds and swamps, tundra, grasslands, coniferous forest, and a deciduous forest. They are told to present their ideas to Wolf executives with detailed drawings and submit a written report.

Students were excited by the memo—"we get to help make a TV show!"—but also felt challenged. The class discussed what they needed to learn and do in order to be successful. Lots of questions came up about the science of ecosystems, which gave Jennifer willing participants in the lessons that followed over the next two weeks. She also gave them plenty of time to work in their teams to brainstorm ideas, do independent research on their ecosystem, and put together their posters and reports. Along the way, students turned in their research notes and rough drafts, and shared their poster outlines with Jennifer and peers for feedback.

Jennifer sprang a surprise as students were finishing up their posters. She handed out an urgent new memo from Wolf TV, giving students an additional task. A test audience wanted more drama in the TV show, so now the set designers needed to decide how a disturbance to their ecosystem—such as a drought, invasive species, or pollution—could challenge the show's contestants. Jennifer used this plot twist to work in some additional science content. It also added a dose of reality by teaching students about the need to react to new developments and think quickly, since that is what can happen in the work world. "It really adds stress," Jennifer notes, "but it's productive stress that ups the quality of their work. It also encouraged student ownership of their products as they realized the extent of the devastation that could possibly destroy everything they spent time building."

Reflecting on the Project

Students showed their posters and explained their ideas in formal presentations to the class and their teacher. It was clear that they had learned a great deal about the science of ecology and had taken care in the creation of their posters. Jennifer also noticed, during presentations, how students began to realize that biomes are somewhat interdependent as well as independent. The written reports provided additional evidence that students had learned the material well.

After the project, Jennifer was proud of its success:

"Most if not all of my intended standards were reached. I am proud of the in-depth knowledge the students gained by completing this project. And my students really bought into the project's scenario. I have kids come up to me two and three years afterward asking when that show will be on the air!"

Project #5: American Archetypes

(11th grade U.S. History)

THE PROJECT IN BRIEF

Project Title: American Archetypes

Project Author: David Ross, (formerly at) Napa New Technology High School, CA

Subject Area: U. S. History

Grade level: 11th

Duration: 20 hours of class time

Driving Question: Do the dominant character archetypes in U.S. history (the Cowboy, the Native American, the slave, the Puritan, etc.) still embody our values?

Project Summary: Students become marketing teams for major food corporations who are asked to review their corporation's choice of an archetypal character to sell their product (Puritan Oil, Calumet Baking Soda, Marlboro cigarettes, Aunt Jemima syrup, etc.). Students research the historical features of their group's archetype and then determine if that archetype is appropriate for the values of modern America and attractive to consumers. Each team presents its findings and recommendations to a panel of community members.

Major Student Products: Research report, supermarket customer survey, oral presentation with PowerPoint slides.

For More Information: Contact David at **david@bie.org**

How the Project Was Conceived and Planned

When David Ross was a sixth-grade social studies teacher in urban Southern California he drifted away from teaching history using traditional methods and in chronological order, because he saw that his students needed to be more engaged. He designed lengthy units focused around a theme or a particular culture and which involved a series of activities that appealed to various learning styles. When he moved to a high school with an intensive school-wide emphasis on Project Based Learning, David realized that while he had been doing pretty successful activity-based teaching, it was not rigorous, inquiry-driven, 21st century skills-focused PBL. He also faced an array of 11th grade standards and the newly demanding tests his students would take each spring, so he knew he needed to step it up a notch.

> Driving Question: Do the dominant character archetypes in U.S. history still embody our values?

In a summer curriculum-writing session at his new school, David began planning projects by exploring the California 11th grade U.S. History standards. He noted he should begin the year with a review of the time periods his students had (supposedly) learned about in 5th and 8th grade. This meant everything from the colonial era to the industrial revolution. So the content decision for his first project was easy. But he knew he couldn't just lecture or assign textbook chapters to "cover" (as opposed to *teach*) the material. Coming up with an interesting project that asked students to review history via inquiry was the hard part of his job.

A conversation with two friends who work in the marketing department of a large company led to an "ah-ha" moment when an idea for a project came to David in a flash. He would ask his students to work as marketing teams and analyze common grocery items that featured the image of icons from America's history such as cowboys, Native Americans, slaves, and Puritans. In doing so, students would be thinking about the role of these people and reviewing several major events and developments in over 200 years of American history. David happily returned to the curriculum writing session the next day, where he penciled in the details of a three-week project that was christened *American Archetypes*.

How the Project Was Managed

Once the project was launched with a mock memo from the boss of a market research company, students did much of the required review on their own. They knew they had to present a recommendation to a panel of adults who would listen to them provide economic and historical reasons why a company should maintain, update or dump an icon such as the African-American woman we see on the label of Aunt Jemima's syrup or the cowboy in ads for Marlboro cigarettes. Students couldn't make a defendable recommendation unless they understood the historical significance of the image that appeared on the label. To add to their historical analysis, the market researchers also needed to survey people at a local supermarket to ask about what the icons meant to them.

Learning historical content knowledge was not a major problem in the project, since so many resources were available. Students conducted rigorous investigations into history, using textbooks and library books, the Internet, and input from David. David was more worried about real-world connections, so he began to make frequent calls to his friends in marketing to confirm that the tasks he asked of students were authentic. He found marketing specialists in his community who eagerly volunteered their time — by email, phone and in person — to work with students. These same people agreed to be on the panel when students presented their analyses and recommendations.

No one was more nervous than David when public presentations began. His students appeared at school that day wearing dresses or suits and ties. Amazingly, the boys even tucked in their shirts. David gave each panelist a handout that included an executive summary of the project and offered a few sample questions in case they got stuck for ideas. The first group was called to the front of the room, turned on the LCD projector and showed their first PowerPoint slide. They gave handouts to the panel and began to talk. And so it went, group after group, for two exhausting but exhilarating days.

Reflecting on the Project

The results were not perfect but students hit nearly all of the outcomes David targeted. Students worked effectively in groups, asked good questions and found their own answers, and presented their work effectively. Some of the students responded well to the questioning by the panel and others revealed a lack of preparation. In terms of content knowledge gained, students re-learned a lot of history, as evidenced by reflections students wrote after the project and by the results of the standards-based objective test David gave his students the Monday after the presentations. Perhaps most importantly, the project convinced several classes of finicky high school students that history was engaging and relevant. And they wanted more projects.

After the end of the project, David reflected on its strengths and weaknesses:

"I was pleased at the interaction between my students and the outside professionals who came in to sit in on panels, listen to the presentations and then question students. It really raised the level of rigor because the students were aware they would be facing people with expertise in the field. Without prompting, students had to study their history so much harder in order to be able to justify their recommendations.

"If anything, my one disappointment came from the level of success we had with group work. All the major student work products were produced collaboratively so it was hard to tell who did what. In the summer that followed the first run of the project I rewrote sections of the project so that there would be more individual accountability."

Project #6: Design and Attract

(11th-12th grade Information Technology)

THE PROJECT IN BRIEF

Project Title: Design and Attract

Project Author: Donita Massing, Miami Valley Career and Technical Center, Dayton, Ohio

Subject Area: Information Technology/Business/Art/Design

Grade level: 11th-12th grade

Duration: 20 hours of class time

Driving Question: How would you devise and develop promotional materials for a specific audience?

Project Summary: Students conduct research and develop marketing materials for a department or program at their school. Each team collects, evaluates, and organizes researched information, identifies target audiences, works within budgets, analyzes the effectiveness of advertising media, and prepares graphics, layouts, and printed materials. Students test-market their products, accept critiques, and make appropriate revisions. The project culminates with a presentation to a panel.

Major Student Products: Oral presentation with a display of marketing materials

For More Information: The Ohio Resource Center: http://pathways.ohiorc.org:80/units.aspx?unit=20

How the Project Was Conceived and Planned

Learning and teaching have come full circle for Donita Massing. When she was an intern in the Teachers in Industry for Educational Support program in Ohio's Miami Valley region she participated in several projects, one of which required her and her classmates to design marketing material for programs at the school.

Despite a seven-year sojourn working in the printing industry, Donita never forgot that wonderful classroom experience. When she returned to education, this time as a Digital Design Instructor, she revived the project for her 11th and 12th grade students. And thus *Design and Attract*, a three-week project that combines technology, business, design, and art was born.

> Driving Question: How would you devise and develop promotional materials for a specific audience?

When she sat down to plan the details of her project, Donita wanted to meet the comprehensive academic and professional requirements included in Ohio's career-technical education (CTE) programs. She also wanted her students to participate, as she did a decade before, in a project that would provide them with skills and experiences that would serve them well in the workaday world. She was in fact seeking a new model for her classroom. "I wanted to provide my students with a relevant project that they could do more independently," she explained. "I was so tired of being the one who was always teaching, who was always providing the answers, the ideas. I wanted my students to do that work."

How the Project Was Managed

Donita kept one thought foremost in her mind during the project: She wanted students to complete the type of work that employees in advertising agencies must do to satisfy clients. She set the stage for this process by having her students read a realistic memo asking them to create marketing collateral and develop an ad campaign for school programs while keeping within the boundaries of a rather modest budget. Working in groups of three, students selected school programs for which to create materials, including brochures, poster boards, websites, audio tracks, TV commercials, and print materials. Each team received help from outside panels, part of the Advisory Board system used in Ohio's CTE programs. Students also tapped the knowledge and skills of other teachers on campus because the project required them to work in a variety of fields — English, business and marketing, art and design.

Donita designed the project to proceed in stages. After the project launched, groups were required to meet and brainstorm a topic and sketch out a design and message, which had to be approved by her before any further work could be done. She asked each group to turn in roughs of their designs for review and drafts of any writing for editing. Even with those checkpoints, Donita later reflected that you can never provide enough "scaffolds" to support students, even for older students experienced with project work. The teams test-marketed their products to check their effectiveness, then made revisions. To culminate their work each team exhibited their marketing materials mounted on poster board, and delivered an extensive oral presentation to a panel of adults that included outside professionals and teaching staff from around the campus.

Reflecting on the Project

According to Donita, her students loved the project as much as she had when she was in their place. Their engagement and effort resulted in high achievement. She received many positive comments from the adults who participated in assessing the students' work. Donita also learned that the successful management of a project can turn on the details, and that's why she now places even more importance on daily feedback to her students about the progress and quality of their work.

Donita noted how well students worked together during the project:

"I was surprised that everything came together so well. I had some problems with groups in the past with kids slacking off. I was surprised at how well they would work together, how the students supported each other during the project and how they encouraged each other to work harder."

GETTING STARTED

This Chapter's Goal

It's time to begin creating your first project. You may make the "big picture" decisions described in this chapter in any order. Some teachers like to start with the content standards they need to teach; others may start by deciding on the scope of the project—how ambitious it will be. Wherever you start, by the end of this chapter you'll have begun the planning process by:

■ Developing an Idea for the Project

■ Specifying Goals for Learning

■ Deciding on the Scope of the Project

■ Writing a Driving Question

✳USE THIS **PROJECT OVERVIEW FORMS**

To keep track of the project you create as you read this book, make a copy of the planning forms we provide in the **Useful Stuff** section (*page 120-121*). An electronic version of these forms is available at **www.bie.org**.

Do I have to be a creative genius?

Don't worry if you've started reading this without having a brilliant idea for a project already in your head. Ideas for projects can come from many sources. Many teachers like to create their own projects from scratch; you can also adapt ideas that have been developed by others.

When you sit and stare at that blank screen or sheet of paper, or when you're ready to begin a brainstorming session with one or more colleagues, you can start from several places. There's no one best place—it's whatever fits your style and whatever works!

Whatever form a project takes, it must have these essential elements to meet our definition of PBL:

- **Significant content**. At its core, the project is focused on teaching students important knowledge and skills, derived from standards and key concepts at the heart of academic content areas.

- **21st century skills**. Students build skills valuable for today's world, such as critical thinking/problem solving, collaboration, and communication, which are taught and assessed.

- **In-depth inquiry**. Students are engaged in a rigorous, extended process of asking questions, using resources, and developing answers.

- **Driving Question**. Project work is focused by an open-ended question that students explore or that captures the task they are completing.

- **Need to know**. Students see the need to gain knowledge, understand concepts, and apply skills in order to create project products, beginning with an Entry Event that generates interest and curiosity.

- **Voice and choice**. Students are allowed to make some choices about the products to be created, how they work, and how they use their time, guided by the teacher and depending on age level and PBL experience.

TIPS FROM THE CLASSROOM

End With a Bang, Not a Whimper

The last day of a project should *not* be, "OK, turn in your papers and here's the test. Our next unit begins Monday." So when you begin developing ideas for projects, envision your students presenting their work to an audience of some sort. Your project should end with a sense of pride, excitement, and celebration.

- **Revision and reflection**. The project includes processes for students to use feedback to consider additions and changes that lead to high-quality products, and think about what and how they are learning.

- **Public audience**. Students present their work to other people, beyond their classmates and teacher.

Places to Start the Wheels Turning

The standards for the course you teach. Ask yourself, do some of the standards I teach require that students learn more than basic knowledge? The more complex standards—those for which students need to show in-depth understanding and/or be able to apply what they're learning—are the best candidates for projects. For example:

- U.S. History Standard: "Analyze the character and lasting consequences of Reconstruction."

  Potential project: Students write and stage a dramatic reading of first-person accounts of life and events during and after Reconstruction.

- Science Standard: "Plan and conduct a scientific investigation to test a hypothesis."

  Potential project: Students analyze soil samples from several locations in the community to determine their chemical makeup and suitability for various uses.

- English/Language Arts Standard: "Compare works that express a universal theme and provide evidence to support the ideas expressed in each work."

  Potential project: Students read various short stories from different cultures, all focused on "leaving home," then use excerpts in podcasts they create to express their own thoughts and feelings about the theme.

- Math Standard: "Move beyond a particular problem by generalizing to other situations."

  Potential project: Students apply linear equations as they make recommendations for the best cell phone plan for a family.

Your community. Ask yourself, is there an issue in our community that merits investigation and perhaps action? These can be the focus of powerful action-oriented projects. For example:

- Issue: The lake is polluted.

  Potential project: Students analyze lake water to identify pollutants, then present findings and make recommendations on how to improve water quality.

- Issue: Traffic is getting worse.

  Potential project: Students measure the volume of traffic and analyze delays on key roadways, then present findings and make recommendations on how to improve traffic flow or reduce traffic.

- Issue: Homeless people are sleeping in the park.

  Potential project: Students read about the issue, visit the park, interview various stakeholders, then write reflections or create art to express a point of view about the situation, for display in the local library or community center.

- Issue: A chain store wants to build on some vacant land.

  Potential project: Students evaluate the pros and cons of allowing the store to build, and stage a debate at the community center.

- Issue: Many people are experiencing health problems such as diabetes.

  Potential project: Students plan a campaign to inform a group of people in the community about the causes, effects, and treatment of diabetes.

What's relevant and interesting to your students. Ask yourself, are my students interested in a current event or a topic relevant to their lives? These topics, although they need to be aligned with important learning goals, are often the most motivating to students. For example:

- Police have been stopping and searching cars driven by teenagers.

  Potential project: Students study the 4th Amendment and precedent cases, interview the police and survey students, then argue the issues in a mock trial.

- A major local employer has closed down.

  Potential project: Students examine the reasons for the closure, predict the effects on the community and recommend action in a presentation to a panel of community members.

- The potential of genetic engineering for changing the human body.

  Potential project: Students decide whether parents should be allowed to have "designer babies" and write bills to present in a mock state legislature.

- The products we buy and their effects on workers and the environment.

  Potential project: Students trace the production of various products they and their families buy, decide if they meet criteria for acceptability, then create a report on the school website.

- The reasons why people fall in love.

  Potential project: Students read fiction and study psychology to develop their own understanding of the topic, then create a multimedia presentation to show to their peers.

What happens in the world outside of school. Ask yourself, what problems or challenges are faced by people in business and industry, the arts, or government? For example:

- Engineers designing bridges.

  Potential project: Students build and test model bridges using their knowledge of math and physics.

- Website designers meeting the needs of clients.

  Potential project: Students interview local small-business owners to assess their needs, then design and propose a website for them.

- Business owners marketing their services and products.

  Potential project: Students in the role of entrepreneurs decide how to develop and promote sustainable tourism in an area.

- Elected officials deciding public policy.

  Potential project: Students propose ideas for spending federal and state funds at the local level.

- Artists finding ways to express an idea.

  Potential project: Students create sculptural models in a design competition for a memorial for Iraq War veterans.

- Scientists advising industry or government

  Potential project: Students study the causes and effects of pine-beetle infestations in forests and propose ways to deal with the problem.

TIPS FROM THE **CLASSROOM**

Name That Project!

Imagine how thrilled your students would be to hear they were starting a project called "The 4th Amendment Project." Now imagine if they'd be more interested in a project called "Can Police Do That to Me?" Or instead of "The Local Geology Project", how about "This Place Rocks!" Or one of the all-time winners: the name of a project on using DNA to solve crimes was, "Blood and Gore All Over the Floor" which you *know* must have intrigued students.

So to help engage students, give your project a catchy name. The name is not, of course, the most important feature of your project design so if it doesn't come to you quickly don't spend too much time on it now—it may occur to you later.

If you'd like to practice, try giving one or more of the **Spotlight Projects** in the front of this book a new name that would be appealing to students.

Finding Ideas from Other Sources

If your brilliant idea battery is running low, another way to jump-start your thinking is to see if other teachers or organizations might have already thought of just the right project for you — or it could be just right, with a few tweaks.

Try these sources:

- **Your colleagues'** file cabinets might contain project ideas — or ideas could be in their heads, if you ask.

- **Online project libraries** have been set up by some states, school districts, school reform networks, and other educational organizations (see *Bulletin Board* on this page for some of our favorites).

- **The teacher's edition of your textbook or other materials from publishers** may contain seeds that can grow into projects.

Bulletin Board

Do You Have Your Virtual Library Card?

Looking for ideas for projects? For a one-stop solution, you can use BIE's Project Search tool at www.bie.org or find links to the following project libraries:

- **Buck Institute for Education and Boise State University:**
  http://www.pbl-online.org/

- **West Virginia Dept. of Education:**
  http://wvde.state.wv.us/teach21/pbl.html

- **Edutopia, from the George Lucas Educational Foundation:**
  http://www.edutopia.org/

- **Envision Schools:**
  http://www.envisionprojects.org

- **High Tech High School:**
  http://www.hightechhigh.org/dc/Projects.php

- **Oracle Education Foundation:**
  http://www.thinkquest.org/

- **WestEd:**
  http://www.wested.org/pblnet/exemplary_projects.html

- **Ohio Resource Center:**
  http://pathways.ohiorc.org/

Specifying Goals for Learning

Know where you're going with this.

Your project should have multiple goals. Some will be drawn from what you have to teach, as stated in your district or state standards. Some goals will come from what you, and perhaps your school, district, and state — and increasingly the business community — believe students need in order to be prepared for life and work. These are often called "21st century skills" such as critical thinking, collaboration, and communication. On the *Project Overview* planning form you'll see a place to indicate which standards and skills you've targeted for your project.

Selecting content standards for your first project:

■ Choose 1-3 standards, depending on how specifically they are written. If you try to include too many standards, you can't teach or assess them well.

■ Go for the "Power Standards." These are the standards that are most important for your students, based on your own analysis or on what your school, district, and/or state have determined. They are often aligned with the items found with higher frequency on state and district standardized tests. For example, if on your state test 10% of the items are about the scientific method, that's a power standard. Or if 5 out of 20 questions on your district's U.S. History assessment are about the Cold War period, that tells you a project on the era might be good way to be sure students learn the material well.

Selecting 21st century skills for your first project:

■ For your first project, we recommend only trying to explicitly teach and assess *two* 21st century skills that are found in all projects: collaboration and presentation. Those are enough for now. See the *Bulletin Board* on page 37 for full descriptions. Well say more about how to teach and assess these skills in the chapters to follow.

■ Another 21st century skill commonly found in PBL is critical thinking/ problem solving, which is also described on the *Bulletin Board* on page 37. For your first project, we recommend designing and managing the project to *encourage* critical thinking and problem solving — but not trying to explicitly teach and assess it, because it's complicated. Save it for later in your PBL career.

- In future projects you can add more or choose other 21st century skills. Although they appear on some lists, be careful about "skills" like "creativity," "perseverance," or "multicultural understanding." Sure, they're wonderful, but hard to actually teach and assess. They're more like personal qualities than skills. It's fine to provide students the opportunity to develop these qualities and attitudes in a project, but can you imagine trying to write a rubric and giving students a score for how well they "demonstrate a global perspective" or "show empathy"?

TIPS FROM THE CLASSROOM

Setting Project Goals Based on What You Personally Value

In addition to content standards and 21st century skills, many teachers like to include goals for PBL that spring from their personal interests or teaching philosophy.

- For example, a teacher may want to enhance the lives of students by helping them develop a sense of their own power to make a difference, see beyond their immediate community, or be able to adapt to a changing world. Projects can be a great way to accomplish these kinds of goals.

- If you are passionate about a topic, activity, or issue and can legitimately tie it to your curriculum, great. That creates enthusiasm that can light up a project. But be careful about making a project your own crusade, for example a political or social issue. Some students (and parents) may resent it if they feel like they're being enlisted in someone else's cause.

21st Century Skills:
More than Text Messaging While Driving

Although 21st century skills may sound like knowing how to download podcasts or find free apps for your cell phone, many educators and business leaders today are talking about the skills people in the post-industrial economy will need in order to thrive.

For more information, see the Partnership for 21st Century Skills at **www.21stcenturyskills.org**.

The Buck Institute for Education describes three of these skills in this way:

Collaboration:

- Takes responsibility for the quality and timeliness of his or her own work; uses feedback; stays on task during group work
- Accepts shared responsibility for the work of the group; helps improve the quality of the work and understanding of other members
- Applies or encourages the use of strategies for facilitating discussion and decision-making
- Manages project by identifying and prioritizing goals and tasks, creating timelines, organizing resources, and monitoring progress
- Respects the ideas, opinions, abilities, values, and feelings of other group members
- Works well with diverse group members
- Encourages group cohesion by using conflict management strategies

Presentation:

- Organizes ideas and develops content appropriate to audiences and situations
- Uses effective oral presentation skills
- Creates media/visual aides that enhance content delivery
- Gauges audience reaction and/or understanding and adjusts presentation appropriately
- Responds to questions appropriately

Critical Thinking and Problem Solving:

- Recognizes and defines problems accurately; raises relevant questions and issues, formulating them clearly and precisely
- Gathers pertinent information from a variety of sources; evaluates the quality of information (source, validity, bias)
- Organizes, analyzes, and synthesizes information to develop well-reasoned conclusions and solutions, judging them against relevant criteria
- Considers alternatives; recognizes and assesses assumptions, implications and practical consequences

Deciding on the Scope of the Project

Imagine the possibilities, but know your limits.

Even though it would be nice to sit in a quiet place all by yourself and plan the most marvelous project on any topic you fancied, and then implement it whenever you wished with all the resources imaginable, with students fully up to the challenge — it's not going to happen. Your context complicates things and may set limits on how ambitious your first project is. Consider the following questions as you develop an idea and decide on the scope of your project:

What requirements do you live with?

- Standards to cover

- Course syllabi and required reading lists

- Standardized, high-stakes tests and other assessments

- The particular mission, a theme, or priorities that everyone in your school, program, or department must address

What time frame do you operate in?

- School/district calendar, including holidays, breaks, special events, and testing

- When you have access to the library, computer lab, or equipment

- If applicable, the availability of community resources and outside-of-school adults

- Your colleagues' timetables if they are involved in your project, or want to schedule their own projects or use resources

What is your classroom like?

- Do you teach in a bright new high-tech heaven, where everyone has a laptop and high-speed access? Does the room have lots of space and moveable tables for group work? If so, great — plan projects to take advantage of it.

- Or do you teach in a small, leaky, thin-walled portable with no windows? Does your room only have two ancient computers, no Internet connection and one dot-matrix printer? Are the desks still bolted to the floor? Don't despair — you can still run very effective projects, but plan them with the constraints in mind.

What are your students like?

- Can they handle sophisticated reading material, do research and write papers, and make oral presentations? Or maybe not yet? You can do Project Based Learning with ALL students — you just need to design and manage projects according to the particular skills, interests, and attitudes of the students you work with each year.

- Are they willing and able to venture out into the community, and do project work outside of school hours?

- Would they be willing to "play along" by taking on a fictitious role in a scenario-based project, or will they respond better to an actual real-world problem-solving situation or a personally relevant topic?

What resources are available to you?

- What human resources could be tapped to help with your project — other teachers, other adults in or outside the school, community organizations, local businesses?

- What material resources do you have access to, if needed — facilities, equipment, technology?

Recommended Scope for Your First Project

A project that is ambitious in scope might last a month or more, even a semester. It would involve multiple subjects and teachers, community outreach, presentations to large public audience, advanced technology… *but you don't need to go there yet*. Get comfortable with the basics of PBL first. Be modest in your first project. Here's what we advise:

- ☑ *2 to 3 weeks in duration (10-15 hours of class time)*
- ☑ *1 curricular area, 1 teacher*
- ☑ *limited complexity and number of student products*
- ☑ *classroom-based, instead of in the community*

Writing a Driving Question

So students always know, "Why are we doing this?"

Sometimes, if you wander into a classroom where students are "doing a project" (i.e., not doing true PBL) and ask them why they are working on a particular task or engaged in an activity, you'll get answers like:

> *"Because the teacher told us to."*

> *"Because we're doing a project about _____ (Ancient Rome; geometry; Romeo and Juliet; photosynthesis; whatever)."*

> *"I don't know."*

A Driving Question for your project should prevent this from happening, because it clearly states the purpose of the project. It gives a focus to all the tasks students do. And because that focus is expressed in the form of a question, it leads students to an inquiry process, and the answer is at the heart of the project's culminating products and performances.

The Driving Question you write now will guide you later as you plan the lessons, resources, and activities that will help your students answer it.

Characteristics of a Driving Question

- **Provocative or challenging** to students, because it is relevant, important, urgent or otherwise interesting.

- **Open-ended and/or complex**; there is no single "right answer," or at least no simple "yes" or "no" answer. It requires in-depth inquiry and higher-level thinking.

- **Linked to the core of what you want students to learn**; to answer it well, students would need to gain the knowledge and skills you have targeted as goals for the project.

How to write a Driving Question

Some Driving Questions are on the abstract side, and writing them takes a little more time and thought; they are similar to what are sometimes called "Essential Questions" in high school reform circles such as the Coalition of Essential Schools. Writing a more concrete or problem-focused Driving Question is relatively straightforward — it typically starts with the words, "How can we…" Just be sure the Question meets the above criteria and you're good to go. The following categories can overlap, so don't get hung up on theoretical purity.

Type of Driving Question:	Examples:
Abstract, Conceptual *(answered by conceptual analysis and logical argument)*	What makes a book a classic? What is a hero? What is justice? When do we grow up? When is war justified? Should U.S. foreign policy be pragmatic or idealistic? Should art be censored? Should President Truman have dropped the atomic bomb on Japan?
More Concrete *(answered mainly by the analysis of empirical evidence)*	Why did the dinosaurs become extinct? Are amusement park rides safe? Is our water safe to drink? Why don't I fall off my skateboard? What effect does population growth have on our society? Can DNA evidence be trusted in criminal trials? Is watching TV beneficial or harmful to teenagers?
Problem-Solving *(answered by offering a reasonable solution)*	How can we decrease the amount of pollutants in the water that runs off our city's streets into the river? How can the federal government use monetary and fiscal policy to address an economic crisis? How can a local business attract more customers? How can we create an effective networking system for a client? How can we improve traffic flow around our school? How can we experimentally and mathematically model a landing sequence like that of the Pathfinder mission to explore Mars?
Design Challenge *(answered by creating — and often executing — a design that effectively meets requirements)*	How can we design a community theatre that meets size limits and seats the most people? How can we build a website to share information and opinions about novels that teenagers might like? How would we design a museum exhibit about the Vietnam War so that it appeals to diverse groups in our community? How can we produce a video of a soap opera in Spanish? How can we create a (work of art/piece of media) to express our thoughts about diversity in our community?

Localize and "Charge" Your Driving Question

Students will find a project more engaging if it **relates to their own lives and communities**. Try to do this when writing your Driving Question, as in these examples:

■ Instead of, "How did World War II affect America?" make it, "Did World War II affect our city the same way it affected other parts of America?"

■ Instead of, "How do architects design environmentally-friendly buildings?" make it, "How could we design an environmentally-friendly building for the property at 5th and Oak Street?"

Likewise, a Driving Question might be even more engaging if it **gives students a "charge" to do something**:

■ Instead of, "What is a healthy diet?" make it, "How can we plan a campaign to raise awareness among various groups in our community about a healthy diet?"

■ Instead of, "How are forests threatened?" make it, "What recommendations would we make about how to improve the health of the forest near our community?"

Before Moving on to the Next Chapter

If you've been using the *Project Overview* form to record your project plans as you moved through this chapter, you should have filled in this much so far:

PROJECT OVERVIEW				page 1
Name of Project:			**Duration:**	
Subject/Course:			**Grade Level:**	
Other Subject Areas to Be Included:				

Project Idea
Summary of the challenge, investigation, scenario, problem, or issue:

Driving Question

Content and Skills Standards to be addressed:

		T+A	E		T+A	E
21st Century Skills explicitly *taught and assessed* (T+A) or *encouraged* (E) by project work, but not taught or assessed:	Collaboration	☐	☐	Other:	☐	☐
	Presentation	☐	☐		☐	☐
	Critical Thinking:	☐	☐		☐	☐

Culminating Products & Performances	**Group:**		**Presentation Audience:** ☐ Class ☐ School ☐ Community
	Individual:		☐ Experts ☐ Web ☐ Other:_____

Let's move on to plan more of your project's details in the next chapter.

PLANNING AND PREPARING

This Chapter's Goal

Now that you've developed an idea for your project, it's time for the details. In this chapter we'll take you through these steps:

1. **Planning:**
   - Summative Assessment: Culminating Products
   - Presentations to an Audience
   - An Entry Event on Day One to Launch the Project
   - Daily Teaching and Learning Tasks
   - Formative Assessment

2. **Creating:**
   - Rubrics
   - Project Calendar, Including Checkpoints
   - Handouts and Other Materials for Students

3. **Deciding:**
   - If and How to Prepare Students for PBL
   - How Student Work Will be Graded
   - How Students Will be Grouped

4. **Arranging:**
   - Resources, Human and Material

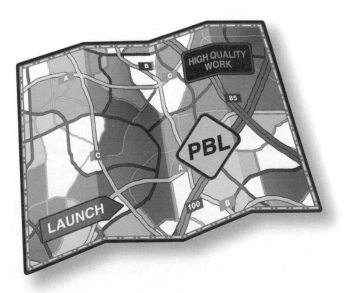

PROJECT PLANNING FORMS

As you work through the steps in this chapter, you will continue to record details about your project on the **Project Overview** form you began to complete in the last chapter.

If you haven't already, make copies of the remaining two **Project Planning Forms** in the back of this (*pages 122-123*) or online at **www.bie.org**.

> ▶ **Project Teaching and Learning Guide**
> ▶ **Project Calendar**

Summative Assessment: Culminating Products

So, where do you want to end up?

Why start by planning the summative assessments for your project? Because it's important to begin with the end in mind. Like taking a journey without a destination, your students will wander aimlessly without clear goals. In the method also known as "backward planning," you start by specifying the content standards and 21st century skills you want students to learn. Then, you decide how you will gather evidence that the goals have been reached—the summative assessment process.

Assessment in PBL requires more than handing out a multiple-choice test supplied by a textbook publisher. To do well in your project, students will need to develop in-depth understanding and apply complex skills which cannot be adequately assessed without complex products. For example, if one of your goals in a Biology class project is for students to deeply understand the concept of natural selection, it would not be enough to simply ask them to recall the definition, or even to explain it in writing—but you would get a more complete picture in, say, a detailed presentation or a panel discussion where students could respond to questions and display their thinking. If your goal is improve students' oral presentation skills, you can only assess that by having students actually make an oral presentation. Less obviously, what if you wanted students to understand how to apply a concept to solve a real-world problem? A short written exercise might give you some data

---

TIPS FROM THE **CLASSROOM**

Keep Project Stuff Together

As you begin to collect materials for your project, including the Project Plan you are creating in this chapter, place all important documents, references, rubrics, assessments, exemplars, etc. in a folder, on your computer and/or in a file drawer—or at least in one pile on your desk.

on how well they can do that, but you might also need to see students perform over time as they create a complex product or solution.

Summative assessment is a two-step process. First you decide what culminating products and/or performances will provide evidence of achievement. Then you decide how to evaluate the products and performances—we'll get to that later in this chapter when we discuss rubrics.

Selecting Culminating Products

The culminating "product" of your project could be a tangible thing students *create*, or it could be a performance—something students *do*. Or you could ask them to do both; for example, write a report and take part in a debate. The key is to align your products with your outcomes, which means making sure you'll be able to find evidence in their work of what you want students to learn. And remember: whatever product(s) you choose, it should be the result of in-depth inquiry, critical thinking, and attention to quality. See the *Bulletin Board* on page 49 for examples of various products.

TIPS FROM THE CLASSROOM

Keep It Real

Try to make your project as authentic as possible.

When you plan the products students will create, imagine what people in the professional world would actually do if they were involved in a similar project. For example, policy analysts for local government would not write an essay to recommend a solution to a community problem. They would probably deliver a memo, report, and/or an oral presentation with slides. A scientist would not create a brochure after conducting an experiment or study—he or she would write an article, report or make a presentation at a conference.

Assessing Content Knowledge

As we said in the **Introduction** to this book, some educators have the misconception that PBL is the "dessert" rather than the main course. And as such, PBL has been dismissed by some as inappropriate for assessing content knowledge. If PBL is not done well, there could be some truth to these charges. So be sure you give proper weight to content knowledge when you create rubrics and coach students in developing culminating products.

And just to make sure you're assessing students' factual knowledge adequately, it's fine to use a traditional summative assessment of content, such as a test or essay, in addition to the culminating products.

For more guidance on assessing individual students' content knowledge when your project involves a product created by a group, see page 94-97 in the **Managing Your Project** chapter.

Assessing 21st Century Skills

In your first project, we recommend a summative assessment of students' collaboration and presentation skills — that's enough for now. In later projects, as you gain competence and confidence in PBL, you can assess other 21st century skills such as critical thinking, problem solving, and project management. (On the *Project Overview* planning form in this book you'll see a place to include these additional skills in future projects. For now, check "E" to indicate that you will design and manage your project to *encourage* these skills, but not formally assess them. Check "T+A" to indicate that you will actually *teach and assess* collaboration and presentation skills.)

Why have summative assessments of 21st century skills? For a couple of reasons:

■ Students are more motivated to do well if they know they are being assessed and will get a score or grade.

■ You will be able to determine how your students are doing: where they might need more support, more time, or different strategies for building their skills.

Summative assessment strategies for 21st century skills:

■ *Presentation rubric*: When students show their work to an audience, include a row in your rubric or use a separate rubric (such as the one provided in **Useful Stuff**) to assign a score and provide you and students with specific information about strengths and weaknesses.

■ *Collaboration rubric*: At the end of the project, ask students to use a rubric (such as the one provided in **Useful Stuff**) to assess and report on how well their group worked together. (For more guidance on how to do this, see the **Reflect and Perfect** chapter.)

■ *Journals or learning logs*: Have students keep a record of their use of skills such as collaboration, critical thinking, problem solving, and project management. You and they can check the evidence at the end of the project and draw conclusions.

■ *Self-Report*: Have students individually write a short report or answer questions about how well they used 21st century skills, referring to a rubric or another set of evaluative criteria. (For more guidance on how to do this, see the **Reflect and Perfect** chapter.)

■ *Peer report*: Have students individually write a short report or answer questions about how well their peers in a group used 21st century skills. You can compare this with their self-reports (and your own observations) to help verify accuracy. (For more guidance on how to do this, see the **Reflect and Perfect** chapter.)

Bulletin Board # Examples of Culminating Products

The following products could culminate your project, or be part of a "package" of products.

Written Products	Presentation Products	Technological Products	Media Products
Research report	Speech	Computer database	Audio recording
Narrative	Debate	Computer graphic	Slide show
Letter	Play	Computer program	Video
Poster	Song/lyric	Web site	Drawing
Brief	Musical piece	Graphic presentation	Painting
Proposal	Dance	Flow chart	Collage
Poem	Oral report		Painting
Outline	Panel discussion		Sculpture
Brochure	Dramatic reenactment		Map
Autobiography	Newscast		Collage
Essay	Discussion		Scrapbook
Book review	Data display (e.g., chart)		Oral history
Report			Photo album
Editorial	Exhibition of products		
Script			

Construction Products	Planning Products
Physical model	Proposal
Consumer product	Estimate
System	Bid
Machine	Blueprint
Scientific Instrument	Flow chart
Museum exhibit	Timeline

Reprinted from the PBL Handbook (2003 Buck Institute for Education), adapted from work by John Thomas

An Engaging Project Launch

Start with a bang.

On occasion, teachers visit a happy place in their mind where all students are interested in quadratic equations, atomic structure, classic 20th century novels, and the causes of World War One. It's a nice place to visit, but let's get back to reality. Whether we like it or not, many students have to be lured to learning. Perhaps you can remember when you had to study the Bill of Rights — was it a big yawn? You knew it was supposed to be important, but it wasn't to you. You had no *need to know* that stuff, except maybe to do well on the test. But in PBL, students are more motivated to learn the knowledge and skills you've targeted because they recognize they need it for a task that engages and challenges them. This starts with an effective project launch. The project launch shouldn't present answers but pose questions and open possibilities. After a successful launch, students should be willing and ready to begin the work of organizing themselves and their tasks.

The project launch is a two-phase process. The first phase motivates your students with an "Entry Event" on Day One that sparks student interest and ignites curiosity — that's what you need to plan now. The second phase, which follows directly, is when you seize on student interest and curiosity to formally begin the inquiry process — we'll explain how to do that in the next chapter, **Managing Your Project**.

TIPS FROM THE CLASSROOM

How to NOT Engage Students at the Start of a Project

If you want to kill students' interest and excitement, start a project by dumping an intimidating "project packet" on their desks at Minute One on Day One, with lots of reading material and detailed explanations of the required work, due dates, total points, and so on. Unless your project is about an exceptionally engaging topic, it will appear to students like just another assignment — except longer, harder, and more stressful. Save the details until *after* students are engaged.

How Can You Spark Students' Interest on Day One?

The Entry Event can take many forms:

- Give students a piece of correspondence (real or fictitious) presenting a challenge

  (Real) A memo from the school principal asks students to plan an "Olympics Day" event for the student body.

  (Fictitious) An email message from the CEO of a business to employees describes a need and asks for proposals (see the sample on page 53).

- Have a discussion about an issue of interest or events in the news

  After a recent plane crash in the area, students discuss how it could have happened, leading to a project focused on the physics of flight.

- Review a website

  Students visit various websites where teenagers can find book recommendations, leading to a project in which they design and create content for a website they think would be more effective.

- Invite a guest speaker

  A representative of the regional visitor's bureau asks the class for help with promoting local attractions to various groups of potential tourists.

- Go on a field trip

  Students visit a nearby shoreline and take note of the amount and type of litter they see, which generates interest in taking action to reduce it.

- Conduct a demonstration or activity

  Students play various card games and speculate about their chances of winning, leading to a project involving probability.

- Show a video or scenes from a film, fictional or documentary

  Scenes from a documentary on the Tuskegee Airmen builds student interest in a project about civil rights and integration in the military.

- Read something provocative

  The Ray Bradbury short story "All Summer in a Day" (in which a child in a colony on Venus is locked in a closet by peers on the only day of sunshine in seven years) kicks off an English class project about being an outcast.

- Present a startling set of statistics or a puzzling problem

  Data showing the rapid spread of and number of deaths from influenza during the pandemic of 1918-19 raises students' concerns about the potential threat from new viruses at the start of a biology project.

- Display photographs or works of art or play a song

  A montage of slides showing art and fashion from the 1960s, set to music from the decade, leads to a project about how art reflects and influences changes in society.

Writing an Effective Piece of Fictitious Correspondence for an Entry Event

If you write a "memo from the boss" (or a letter, email, text message, etc. from whomever) to launch your project, here's how to make it most effective:

- **Make it sound authentic.** Imagine how the person writing it would actually talk—what tone they would take, the vocabulary, slang or jargon they might use, and the amount of information they would include.

- **Make it look authentic.** Use the font and format that would really be used for the type of correspondence. Include a letterhead or logo if appropriate—a real one or one you fake.

- **Make the situation clear.** Give students an understanding of their role and the problem they need to solve or the need they are addressing.

- **Make the task clear.** Tell students what they need to do and create. Mention what products are expected, with some information about the content and process, and tell students that they will be presenting their work.

- **Make it sound important and urgent.** Let students know the stakes involved, that they are being counted upon, why their good work is needed.

- **Make it short.** Do not include as many details as you would on a typical "major assignment sheet" handout. Let a few things remain unstated, so students will ask questions.

The Memo that Launches
the "A Balancing Act" Spotlight Project

Wolf Broadcasting Company

To: Set Design Teams
From: Robert Merdock, Head of Programming
Re: Biosphere Series

After review of Nielsen television ratings season after season, we understand that the popularity of reality TV is not dying out. It is time for us to jump on board. We here at Wolf Studios are very excited about our new reality TV series idea, now going into development. Seeing the success for multiple seasons of the CBS series "Survivor," we at Wolf Studios would like to develop our own concept, "Beating the Biosphere."

On our series, contestants will have to compete in games to earn points in order to keep the "privilege" of staying in the biosphere each week and receiving cash rewards. The player with the fewest points will have to return home.

The biosphere itself will be a replica of the earth's natural environment. It will be a 7,200,000-cubic-foot sealed glass and space-frame structure and contain 8 biomes, including a 900,000-gallon ocean, a rain forest, a desert, fresh water ponds and swamps, tundra, grasslands, coniferous forest, and a deciduous forest area. Your job is to design the self-sustaining "set" of each ecosystem.

Present your ideas to me and our production team leaders with some detailed large-scale drawings and a written report about your ecosystem. Since we have limited space in the biosphere, how about picking one example of a biological community that you think might work best in your set.

It will take all of our efforts together to make this new venture happen. The quality of your work is key to our success — and to your continued employment. I look forward to hearing from you asap.

Presentations to an Audience

Showtime!

Presentation of student work to an audience is one of the essential features of PBL for several reasons. One reason is obvious — to give students practice in 21st century skills such as oral communication, using presentation media, and critical thinking as they anticipate and answer questions from a particular audience. Another reason is psychological — students are more motivated to do high-quality work if they know it will be seen by someone besides their teacher and their usual classmates. And in many projects, the goal is to persuade or communicate, which obviously requires an audience of some sort. Finally, there's a celebratory and "public relations" reason. After all their hard work in a project, a presentation is a nice opportunity for students to shine in front of people in the school and community.

Who Will See Students' Work?

Because this is your first project, we suggested not being overly ambitious when you decided the scope in the **Getting Started** chapter, and this includes the audience for student presentations. The logistics of arranging public demonstrations of learning can get complicated, and the quality of student work the first time around might not be where you want it to be. And especially if this is your students' first experience with PBL, they might be a little *too* stressed if you tell them you've invited their parents, some local professors, the city council, "and oh, by the way, the presentation will be a live webcast seen by thousands all over the state."

Potential audiences for student presentations in your first project:

- *Other students at school*. Your students can make presentations in other classrooms or to other students invited into yours, display their work on campus, present at special events like assemblies, or distribute publications.

- *Other adults at school*. Invite administrators, other teachers, counselors, librarians, and staff members into your classroom.

- *Other adults who visit the school*. If appropriate for your project, and you and your students are ready, invite parents, school district personnel or board members, experts, community members, business representatives, or local officials.

Avoid Death by Repetitive Presentations

Imagine sitting through eight presentations on the exact same topic. Perhaps you don't need to imagine it — you and your students have had the soul-draining experience. Plan your project to enable students to vary their presentations and learn from each other's work.

- Make sure the project is truly open-ended — with several possible answers to a Driving Question or solutions to a problem — to ensure that you will see varied presentations.

- Under the umbrella of the same Driving Question, have students read different books that share a common theme, explore different examples of the same concept, or study different times, events, and places with a common focus.

- Distribute tasks or topics so that each group is responsible for one part of the project, e.g., in a project to recommend solutions to noise pollution in the community, each group studies a different source of noise.

- Assign students different roles or perspectives from which to provide answers to a Driving Question (e.g., when presenting views on a controversial issue, have students take the roles of various stakeholders).

How Will Students Interact with People Who See Their Work?

Your students should not simply present their work, then retreat into the shadows. They should interact in some way with their audience. Even if students are simply standing next to something they've created, and not actually making a formal presentation, make sure they talk with people who have come to see it. Or if students have distributed something they've written, at least have them collect feedback from readers.

If students are presenting to an audience, they should be questioned about their knowledge and asked to explain choices, describe processes, make connections and predictions, recognize implications. This is another way for students to show they learned the content and can use 21st century skills like critical thinking and problem solving. A question-and-answer session can also be a key part of your assessment strategy, by allowing you to probe for individual knowledge and understanding.

What audience members could do:

- Listen, look, and ask questions (then applaud!)

- Play a role when asking questions, e.g., pretend they are the clients for whom students have developed a product or done a service, or stakeholders hearing proposals on an issue

- Review student work and evaluate it, either by offering comments aloud or by writing on a form or survey

✳ USE THIS A U D I E N C E   F E E D B A C K   F O R M   *(page 131)*

Daily Teaching and Learning Tasks

You can't go have coffee while students work.

At this point you have the end of your project (the culminating products and presentations), and you have the beginning (the Entry Event on Day One). Now it's time to plan what goes in between. As you can tell by now, planning a project is different than planning a sequence of activities. Activities can be planned on a daily basis, even the night before class or during early-morning prep when the copy room is abuzz with flying paper. Don't try that with a project, because it all has to hang together; the tasks you plan must fit into the organizing structure the project provides.

Planning the day-to-day use of time is one of the trickiest parts when you first try PBL. Daily teaching and learning tasks will include a mix of independent student work, teacher-guided activities, and, at times, good ol'-fashioned direct instruction — all wrapped up in the context of the project.

Plan Backwards from Culminating Products and Assessments

A good way to plan your project's daily teaching and learning is to "unpack" the knowledge and skills students will need in order to do well on the project's major products, performances, and assessments. For example, if students had to write a report and make an oral presentation about the design of an ecosystem for a biosphere, as in our "A Balancing Act" Spotlight Project, you could imagine a fairly long list of terms and concepts they'd have to understand. Add to this the skills of researching, writing, making a presentation, and creating visual aides. After you have such a list, you can plan how students are going to get the information they need, whether it is from a textbook, the library, a lesson you provide, an outside expert, or the Internet. We've created a simple two-column chart called a "Project Teaching and Learning Guide" to help you organize these lists. See the completed example on page 58 from the "American Archetypes" Spotlight Project.

PROJECT TEACHING AND
LEARNING GUIDE *(blank form page 122)*

✳ USE THIS

Common Questions About Daily Teaching and Learning in PBL

Q: **Do I just turn students loose once the project starts?**

A: *No, you still need to plan how time will be used each day, while allowing for some flexibility. There should be a mix of direct instruction and other lessons, opportunities to practice skills, and independent work time, all directed toward answering your project's Driving Question. You may also need to provide resources to students, or at least help them find resources.*

Q: **How do I mix lessons with independent project work time?**

A: *It depends on the nature of your project, your students, and your own style. Most class periods should include some time for project work, or at least some time to think about and discuss how a lesson applies to the project. If, after a series of lessons, you tell students, "OK, now apply all this to your project" and they say, "What project?" then you'll know you've gotten the mix wrong.*

Q: **I'm a good lecturer, so can I still do that in PBL?**

A: *Of course students appreciate the melodious sound of your voice, your wit and charm, your fascinating anecdotes and wise, provocative ideas. But during a project resist the urge to talk for five straight days. There are times when a short lecture may be the best way to give students information they need. Just make sure students see the lecture within the context of the project and understand that it will help them complete their tasks. Better yet, wait until students ask a specific question or realize they need certain information before you take the podium.*

Q: **Can I still use traditional tools like textbooks, worksheets, homework, and quizzes?**

A: *Yes you can—as long as students don't wonder, "Why are we doing this?" It should be obvious that any task they do will help them answer the Driving Question and successfully complete the project. Remember—in PBL, the project is what organizes the use of traditional teaching tools.*

Spotlight Project Sample: *American Archetypes*

PROJECT TEACHING AND LEARNING GUIDE

Project: American Archetypes

Course/Semester:

Knowledge and Skills Needed by Students to successfully complete culminating products and performances, and do well on summative assessments	Scaffolding / Materials / Lessons to be Provided by the project teacher, other teachers, experts, mentors, community members
Business communication	↑ Students write resumes and cover letters — instruction, including samples and templates, provided by counselor (peer editing of drafts, final edits by counselor
Online research skills	↑ Evaluating website accuracy activity (online and worksheet). Effective search (engine) techniques activity led by teacher
PowerPoint and Excel	↑ Instruction in software use provided by computer applications teacher
Marketing tools and techniques	↑ Weekly visits by local business partners with expertise in marketing and product development. Students begin email exchanges with experts.
Presentation skills	↑ Video review of students presentations Mock presentation by instructor Jigsaw activity to learn presentation rubric Peer assessment (using rubric) of practice presentations
Report writing	↑ Direct small-group instruction on the features of report writing by instructor. Peer editing of drafts, final drafts by teacher. Direct small-group instruction on MLA Citations (including online bibliography generators). Jigsaw activity to learn report writing rubric
U.S. history content knowledge	↑ Textbook review, lectures, research-based worksheets, objective weekly quizzes, online research

Formative Assessment

How am I doing, coach?

It's an old story in PBL...

> *The teacher launched the project with a bang, the kids have been busy for two weeks researching the topic and preparing PowerPoint slides with their answer to the Driving Question, and now it's time for the big finish. The papers are turned in and oral presentations are made to an audience. But after the last presentation ends, audience members applaud politely but briefly and offer comments like, "they sure seemed engaged" and "lots of effort, for sure!" The teacher smiles weakly but feels uneasy — many presentations were too long, too short, too boring, or just plain unorganized. The slides were a mishmash. That weekend, as the teacher reads the papers, a sinking feeling sets in. The papers wander off topic... full of mistakes... seems like one person in some groups did all the work... not enough sources... superficial understanding... And the teacher wonders, "Did I just waste two weeks?"*

Any clue about what was missing in this picture? That's right — the use of assessment practices throughout the project that would have provided information and guidance as students "formed" their work. Your students need feedback on their progress. Feedback works best if it's immediate and detailed. Think about basketball practice or piano lessons. Your coach or instructor doesn't wait two weeks to let you know you turned your wrist too far while shooting a free throw or hit the wrong note.

The results of formative assessment may reveal the need to provide more support or adjust your project plan. Of course, you're informally checking student understanding and progress on tasks all the time, by observing your classroom and talking with students. But be sure to plan more formal, regular opportunities — early, midway, and late in your project — to gather information, diagnose problems, and take corrective action.

How to Conduct Formative Assessment

- **To assess content knowledge and understanding,** have students take a quiz, do a quick-write to explain a concept, or complete an individual homework assignment.

- **To assess specific skills** students need for project work — such as using technology or equipment, writing, graphic design, using math, recording data — have them practice so you can give feedback.

- **To assess the quality of student work, including inquiry skills**, review interim products such as:
  - ▶ Lists of questions they are investigating
  - ▶ Resource lists and research notes
  - ▶ Concept maps
  - ▶ Rough drafts
  - ▶ Learning logs or journals
  - ▶ Plans, prototypes, preliminary drawings
  - ▶ Website maps
  - ▶ Storyboards for videos or PowerPoint slides
  - ▶ Practice presentations

- **To assess 21st century or "process" skills** such as collaboration, observe groups as they work, talk with group members, or hold meetings with group leaders. To find out if students are managing time and tasks well, have them turn in status reports on task completion.

Rubrics

Make it easier for you, clearer for students.

The complex products and presentations found in PBL must be guided and evaluated using carefully designed assessment practices. A general or vague description of what you expect, or even a slightly more specific checklist, is just not going to cut it. To provide students with clear criteria for their work, and to allow you to assess it efficiently and thoroughly, we recommend a detailed analytic rubric. This type of rubric is usually written in the form of a table that describes what various levels of quality work look like, along several dimensions. (The examples we provide in **Useful Stuff** are analytic rubrics.)

Three key points to remember about rubrics in PBL:

- Each culminating product or performance in your project will need its own rubric.

- Assess content knowledge separately from 21st century skills such as collaboration and presentation, either by having separate rows in one rubric, or if this gets too complicated, by having two or three separate rubrics. See the sample content rubric on page 61.

Spotlight Project Sample: *A Balancing Act*

RUBRIC FOR CONTENT KNOWLEDGE AND UNDERSTANDING

Criteria	Developing (*does not meet performance standards*)	Proficient (*meets performance standards*)	Advanced (*exceeds performance standards*)
Part I — Poster and First Written Report			
Completeness and Accuracy of Required Information: ▶ Where in the world the ecosystem would be found	One or more pieces of required information are omitted.	All required information is included.	All required information is included.
▶ Biological community containing at least 2 producer species, 3 consumer species, and 1 example of each of the symbiotic relationships (mutualism, commensalisms, and parasitism) ▶ Range, population size, mating rituals, and nutritional requirements of each species ▶ Drawing of food web showing position of each species in it ▶ Usefulness or attractiveness of each species to humans ▶ Any threats each species faces ▶ Climate: annual temperature ranges, seasons, average annual precipitation, latitude, and humidity ▶ Surface conditions: soil minerals, soil texture, water sources, landscape ▶ Abiotic features that help to sustain the ecosystem	Significant information is incorrect, key terms are used inappropriately, and/or important details are missing.	Most significant information is correct, although there are some minor errors or missing details.	All information is correct and discussed in detail.
Understanding of Concepts: ▶ The "balance" that makes an ecosystem self-sustaining ▶ Limiting factors on a population ▶ Carrying capacity of an ecosystem	Explanation is not complete, clear, accurate, and/or detailed.	Explanation is generally complete, clear, accurate, and detailed.	Explanation is complete, clear, accurate, and detailed. Explanation shows evidence of sophisticated understanding (e.g., use of analogies, examples, complex vocabulary).
Part II — Second Written Report			
Understanding of Concepts: ▶ Potential effects of introducing a nonnative species into an ecosystem ▶ How environmental factors can impact survival of a population ▶ Potential consequences of human activities on an ecosystem ▶ How an ecosystem can be restored to balance after a disturbance	Explanation is not clear, accurate, and/or detailed.	Explanation is generally clear, accurate, and detailed.	Explanation is clear, accurate, and detailed. Explanation shows evidence of sophisticated understanding (e.g., use of analogies, examples, complex vocabulary).

- Show the rubrics to students early in the project, to guide their work. Make sure they understand the rubric thoroughly, ideally by comparing it to an exemplar of the kind of work they are supposed to produce. You could post the rubric on the wall, keep copies in a Project Center in the classroom, make it available online, and even send it home for parents to see.

✱USE THIS RUBRICS FOR COLLABORATION AND PRESENTATION (*pages 124-125*)

Bulletin Board Writing Righteous Rubrics

The language in a rubric should be clear and specific. Avoid terms like "excellent" or "interesting" that could mean different things to different people. Make sure students can understand the rubric.

The best way to write a rubric is to look at actual samples of student work, of varying levels of quality. This helps you write very detailed and concrete descriptions. If you don't have samples yet, you'll need to draw from what you know about the quality of work you expect, or by using samples from other sources, including professionals.

Give more weight to some categories when appropriate. For example, in a core academic course content knowledge should count for more than how nice the collage looks (this would differ in an art class).

Don't rely solely on online rubric-writing tools. Although they can be a good place to start, their "boilerplate" style usually means you'll have to add more descriptive language.

Standards documents from your state, district, or national organizations often contain language you can import into your rubrics.

A Project Calendar

If you're not the organized type, you will be now.

In the **Getting Started** chapter you reviewed your school's annual calendar and chose an appropriate window during which your project can run. Now, as you're planning the details of your project, create a calendar to keep track of how you'll implement it on a daily basis. After the project is launched, you could share the calendar with students too.

A Project Calendar is pretty simple — you can use your own, or use the blank one you may have copied from the back of this book. You can see a sample on page 64 of a completed Project Calendar from one of our Spotlight Projects.

PROJECT CALENDAR FORM (*page 123*)   **✳ USE THIS**

Record the following on your calendar:

☑ *The Entry Event on Day One that launches the project*

☑ *Daily teaching and learning tasks, including formative assessment*

☑ *Checkpoints for completion of project tasks*

☑ *Presentation schedule*

☑ *Due dates for culminating products*

☑ *Tests or other summative assessments*

☑ *Time for reflection and celebration at the end of the project*

"A rookie error of epic proportions"

David remembers a hard-earned lesson about the need for checkpoints from the first time he ran the *American Archetypes* project:

"I set a due date for final reports on the day that presentations were scheduled to begin. I didn't require my groups to turn in any planning documents for their Power Point presentations. I didn't require my groups to submit drafts of written reports. The work was mostly atrocious.

"I noticed a flurry of action the day of presentations. In one corner, three students hovered over a group member who was madly creating PowerPoint slides on the fly. No one had time to review the work being done, which featured 12 fonts, 5 background colors, 7 transitions and the occasional misspelling of the word 'the.' In another corner of the room three more students were shoving notes, printouts and textbooks at a teammate who was the 'writer' for the group. No one had time to edit the report, which featured an alarming number of errors.

"After that debacle I scheduled all written work, models, and electronic presentations to be turned in the Friday prior to presentations, which gave me time to assess the work and provide feedback."

Spotlight Project Sample: *Design and Attract*

PROJECT CALENDAR

Project: Design and Attract | **Start Date:** Feb. 2

PROJECT WEEK ONE

MONDAY	TUESDAY	WEDNESDAY	THURSDAY	FRIDAY
Entry Event: memo from Middleburg University	Explanation of Project Details, Procedures	Design Software review (taught prior to project)	Lesson: Design theory	Checkpoint: Quiz on Design Theory
Know/Need to Know list	Explanation of rubrics for major products	Lesson: Assessing client needs	Team work time: continue assessment of client needs; begin brainstorming ideas for materials	Team work time: begin design of materials
Project Teams Announced	Review samples of professional products in relation to rubric	Team work time: begin assessment of client needs	Homework: complete client needs assessment (due mon)	Review/Revise Know/Need to Know list
Discussion of expectations for team work	Team meeting: task list	Homework: Reading on assessing client needs	Daily team assessment	Daily team assessment; meeting with team leaders
First team meeting: roles, contract, initial task list	Daily team assessment	Daily team assessment		

PROJECT WEEK TWO

MONDAY	TUESDAY	WEDNESDAY	THURSDAY	FRIDAY
Checkpoint: collect "Client Needs Assessment"	Checkpoint: Collect notes on initial ideas for materials	Lesson: Typography review	Checkpoint: Quiz on typography	Checkpoint: Teams meet with others to critique work in progress
Team work time: Continue designing materials	Checkpoint: Teams meet with others to critique work in progress	Team work time: Continue creating materials	Explanation of rubric for presentation of products	Team work time: Continue creating materials, planning presentation
Homework: notes on initial ideas due tomorrow	Team work time: discuss feedback from critique	Review/revise Know/Need to Know list	Team work time: Continue creating materials	Daily team assessment
Daily team assessment	Daily team assessment	Daily team assessment	Daily team assessment; meeting with team leaders	Homework: Continue creating materials

PROJECT WEEK THREE

MONDAY	TUESDAY	WEDNESDAY	THURSDAY	FRIDAY
Team work time: Finish creating materials, planning presentation	Team work time: Prepare and practice presentation of materials	Team work time: Prepare and practice presentation of materials	Presentation Day	Self and Peer Assessment
Checkpoint: Submit materials for teacher review	Daily team assessment	Daily team assessment		Project Debrief and celebration
Final review/revision of Know/ Need to Know list				
Daily team assessment				

PBL STARTER KIT / **PLANNING AND PREPARING** / **65**

Handouts and Other Materials for Students

Don't spend Monday morning at the copier.

As we said earlier, do not dump a big "Project Packet of Materials" on students' desks on Day One or you might cancel out the motivating effect of your Entry Event by making the project look too intimidating. However, you will need to have handouts ready when students need them, so create them now and have copies made before launching the project.

Must-have handouts:

- Rubrics for each major product
- Rubrics for 21st century skills
- Project Management Log: Group Tasks
- Project Group Contract
- Project Work Report: Individual
- Project Work Report: Group

✱USE THIS You can find handout masters of all the above (*pages 124-129*), except for the specific rubric for each major product which you'll have to create yourself.

Optional handouts:

- Project Calendar or other graphic organizer of project steps and checkpoints
- A summary of the project, which may include information on major products, how work will be done, grading policy, due dates, etc.
- Resource list showing readings, websites, people or organizations to contact, etc.
- Research log or other record of how students spend their time, on what tasks, using what resources, etc.
- Note-taking guide or other scaffolds to help students record what they learn

Other materials, depending on your particular project, may include:

- Readings or other content-related written materials
- Exemplars of products
- Guidelines, templates or other scaffolds for creating products
- Materials to accompany lessons

If and How to Prepare Students for PBL

Tune your engine before hitting the road

Project Based Learning is different. You know that, but your students may not. Before starting the first project, you may have to prepare them for what is to come, in terms of both the skills they will need and the classroom culture they can expect. By "culture" we mean the beliefs, attitudes, ways of doing things, and the overall spirit shared by students and teacher—we'll say more about how to create this in your classroom in the **Managing Your Project** chapter that follows. Here in **Planning and Preparing**, we'll look at some ways to build the skills students will need for PBL.

Two Words: Independence and Inquiry

There are lots of other words we could emphasize as key to effective PBL: authenticity, relevance, rigor, responsibility. But for now, let's focus on the two "I's"—independence and inquiry.

By *independence*, we mean that students are able to work without relying on the teacher too much. They can take the initiative, stay on task, find resources, learn from each other, and solve problems.

By *inquiry*, we mean that students are asking, investigating, and answering questions as they build their knowledge and skills.

Especially if PBL is new to students, creating a culture of independence and inquiry is hugely important. You can't expect students accustomed to traditional education to suddenly be able to meet the demands of PBL. Imagine how it might feel to a student who has always sat passively at his or her own desk, trying to absorb information delivered by the teacher, reading assigned textbook chapters, filling out worksheets, memorizing for a test. Now you're asking that student to think about a Driving Question that has no single right answer, to ask questions themselves, to find resources, to work collaboratively, to present and defend ideas to an audience.

Even a student who has experienced classes with activities like science labs, group problem-solving exercises, lively discussions, Internet research tasks, and presentations of student work could find PBL to be challenging. Because even though a PBL-oriented classroom might still make use of all those experiences, it's different. In PBL, the activities and learning have a focus for inquiry—answering the Driving Question—and they are not all directed by the teacher every step of the way. Students need to be prepared for this kind of inquiry and independence. If they are not prepared, it's not pretty. Here's a little story from BIE Director of Professional Development David Ross about what can happen.

> *Several years ago I was asked to provide PBL workshops to a group of high schools in the Seattle area. Because of trouble securing subs, the administrators decided to spread the sessions over several months rather than hold them on the usual back-to-back days. Some teachers were so enthused by what they learned on Day 1 that they decided to write projects on the spot and launch them before I returned to finish the workshop. Big mistake.*

> *A few months later I delivered a second day of PBL training with recommendations on, you guessed it, creating a culture of inquiry and independence. I was confronted during bagels and coffee by two burly history teachers who told me in short order that I was full of you-know-what. Their students had struggled mightily and they had to abort the project. After the project was launched, the students didn't ask questions. They waited for the teachers to tell them what to do next. They did not find resources on their own. They didn't work well in groups. They wasted time. They thought their teachers didn't know what they were doing. These guys did not like feeling incompetent in front of their students. They pulled the plug. I hope they read this book and give PBL a second, better chance. (And next time I'll warn workshop participants to "Wait for Day Two!")*

Building Skills Before and During a Project

You know your students best. Before you launch your project, decide what they can handle and what skills you might need to spend a few days or even weeks building in advance. Consult the following pages for guidance, and see the websites listed for more information. And realize that you may need to reinforce these skills once the project is underway.

If your students need to learn how to **work effectively in groups**

Prepare them *before* a project by having them:

Participate in team-building activities such as games, puzzles, physical activities, model-building challenges

Practice project management, collaboration and cooperation skills in short activities where they learn:

- how to perform various group roles (leader, recorder, materials-keeper, etc.)

- how to use various processes for making decisions (including how to reach consensus)

- how to divide tasks appropriately

- how to assess themselves using a rubric for collaboration

Find information and more ideas online at:

YouthLearn (from the Education Development Center):

http://www.youthlearn.org/learning/teaching/community.asp

Teaching and Learning with Technology Center (Georgia State University):

http://www2.gsu.edu/~wwwltc/howto/enablestudentcollab.htm

eHow (an online service from the business world):

http://www.ehow.com/how_2060519_develop-collaboration-skills. html

---

If your students need to learn how to **think critically, solve problems, and ask good questions**

Prepare them *before* a project by having them:

Practice short problem-solving and critical thinking in activities such as:

- tasks requiring students to make something together (e.g. build a tower of straws; assemble a puzzle; work on anagrams or word puzzles) then discuss how they did it

- open-ended tasks (e.g., think of various possible endings for a story; propose solutions to a problem) then discuss how they did it

Practice how to brainstorm effectively

Practice asking questions or creating a concept map when confronted by a challenging task or topic, a mystery, a problem to solve, etc.

Find information and more ideas online at:

Critical Thinking Consortium:
> http://tc2.ca/

Critical Thinking Community:
> http://www.criticalthinking.org/

Critical Thinking Project (Washington State University):
> http://wsuctproject.wsu.edu/

Mind Tools (from the business world) on problem-solving:
> http://www.mindtools.com/pages/main/newMN_TMC.htm

and on brainstorming:
> http://www.mindtools.com/brainstm.html

YouthLearn, on teaching students how to ask questions:
> http://www.youthlearn.org/learning/teaching/questions.asp

TIPS FROM THE **CLASSROOM**

Teach the Tech Before the Project!

One of the most common pitfalls of PBL is how big a time-suck technology can be.

If it takes students only a few days to learn the content knowledge in a project, but it takes twice that long to learn to use PowerPoint, then things are out of whack. Spend more of the time on the important stuff! And your students don't need the added stress of figuring out a technical problem right before a project deadline.

To avoid this, teach students how to use a new technology, program, or piece of equipment before the project starts.

If your students need to learn **how to present** what they have learned

Prepare them *before* a project by having them:

Learn techniques and tips offered by experts

Analyze and critique videos of past student presentations or analyze a mock presentation by the teacher

Understand the details of a presentation rubric by using it to assess practice presentations

Discuss what it means to be a respectful audience during presentations

Find information and more ideas online at:

Several sites from the business world, such as:

http://www.moneyinstructor.com/publicspeaking.asp

http://lorien.ncl.ac.uk/ming/dept/Tips/present/present.htm

http://www.nwlink.com/~donclark/leader/leadpres.html

http://www.presentationskillshelp.com/

If your students need to learn how to **manage time and tasks**

Prepare them *before* a project by having them:

Plan how they would accomplish a complex task (e.g., take a trip, prepare a meal, or run a small business)

Practice how to use a "Time and Task Log" or other record-keeping system

Find information and more ideas online at:

Mind Tools on project management:

http://www.mindtools.com/pages/main/newMN_PPM.htm

Make It Happen!

http://www.makeithappen.ws/projecttools.shtml

If your students need to learn how to **do research**

Prepare them *before* a project by having them:

Practice research skills with short, simple exercises and assignments using the Internet and print resources

Learn how to use other information-gathering techniques such as interviews, field visits, and surveys

Visit the Library or Media Center to become familiar with what is available to them

Find information and more ideas online at:

AT&T's Knowledge Network Explorer, on 21st Century Literacies:

http://www.kn.pacbell.com/wired/21stcent/index.html

CyberSmart! Education:

http://www.cybersmartcurriculum.org/

LibrarySupportStaff.com, on Information Literacy:

http://www.librarysupportstaff.com/teachlib.html

How Student Work Will be Graded

So you can explain why they only got a B+.

The topic of grading can generate much debate among teachers, and everyone has their own particular way to assign grades or points. You use your own judgment as a professional, with your own set of considerations. So we won't try to tell you exactly how to grade your students in a project. But when a student (or a parent) asks about that all-important letter or point total, you'd better be sure your project had a well-planned, justifiable grading system.

Grading suggestions in PBL:

■ Instead of giving one overall project grade or score, assign a grade or score to *each* product or performance in the project.

Why? Because rolling everything into one project grade hides particular areas of strength and weakness; a student may have written a great report but delivered a so-so oral presentation. If you haven't assigned separate grades, it's harder to give a student specific, timely feedback. It's also harder to explain later, if you're asked about an overall project grade.

- Include a mix of individually-earned grades and group-earned grades in every project, and record them separately in your grade book. Especially when you're new to PBL, play it safe by giving more weight to individual grades.

  Why? Because it's fairer, especially to a strong student in a weak group. It also will save you from arguing about "why my grade is based on what other people did."

- Separate grades or scores for demonstrating 21st century skills from grades for learning subject-matter content.

  Why? Because you'll be able to give both categories the appropriate weight when deciding on a course grade. Also, by reporting them separately, instead of hiding them in a mash-up with other grading criteria, you're raising the importance of 21st century skills in the minds of students and parents.

How Students Will Be Grouped

"Can we work with our friends?"

Although PBL can be done when students work individually — as in many Senior Project programs — we've been emphasizing the importance of building the 21st century skill of *collaboration*. Students can't practice and develop competence in collaboration if you don't embed them in meaningful group work. So plan your project accordingly.

Three strong recommendations about forming project work groups:

- **You**, not students, choose group members.

  Before the launch of the project, you should decide who will be in each group. This allows you to select students who will work well together and bring a range of skills and perspectives to the project. Also, students can waste a great deal of time and much of your energy by negotiating the composition of groups. This process also can lead to social isolation for students who are perceived to be unpopular or who are judged by their peers to have low academic skills.

- **Four** is the most effective size for a group.

  The nature of your project and the student work it involves may dictate the size of your groups. But generally speaking, four is an effective group size because it allows students multiple opportunities to share the workload and practice

If a High-Achieving Student is Concerned About "Doing All the Work" in a Group

This is a common problem in heterogeneous groups. Here are some strategies to handle it:

- Make each group member accountable for turning in some pieces of project work. Assigning individual grades for separate pieces of work will help reinforce the need for responsibility, and reassure high-achieving students.

- When discussing expectations for project work with students, be sure "sharing the workload" is on the list. Remind them that the ability to negotiate issues about balancing the workload among colleagues is a valuable real-world skill.

- Teach groups how to distribute the workload, assign tasks, and stay accountable to each other.

- Help groups recognize that everyone has different skills and can find ways to contribute to a project.

- Let all students know that you will closely observe groups as they work, and intervene if the effort isn't balanced.

interpersonal skills. Three per group could work, or maybe five, but with five or more it is harder to make sure each student contributes to the effort and is not freeloading.

- **Heterogeneous** groups are best.

Include a mix of skills in each group, so each student can find ways to contribute to the group effort. Be sure to place special needs students or those who are not fluent in English with teammates who are understanding and helpful.

To review: a quick quiz on grouping students

When a student asks you the question about working with friends, the correct answer is:

a) No, because I've already assigned everyone to groups for very good reasons, which I'd be happy to explain if you'd like to meet with me after school

b) No, because I've seen things turn ugly when people try to work with friends, who can soon become ex-friends

c) No, because working with different people is what happens in the real world, so it's a good skill to practice

d) All of the above, because that's always the best choice on these tests, right?

Resources, Human and Material

Arrange now and relax later.

Running a project can be a resource-intensive process. You may require material resources such as books, art supplies, and construction materials, and equipment such as LCD projectors, laboratory supplies, and laptops. You may need human resources, including people from the community, other teachers, or experts reached by phone or online. You'll see a place to list these on the *Project Overview* form in **Useful Stuff**. We have only one simple suggestion on this topic:

☑ *Arrange everything well in advance.*

Before Moving on to the Next Chapter

On pages 77-78 you can see a completed Project Overview form, from our "Projectile Motion" Spotlight Project.

If you've been using the *Project Overview* form to record your project plans as you moved through this chapter, you should have filled in every part of it up to "Resources Needed."

TIPS FROM THE CLASSROOM

Don't Carve Your Plan in Stone

Don't get too attached to every detail in your project plan — stay flexible. The path your project takes may change to some extent, because PBL is never fully predictable. You might see the need to make adjustments, and your students might have a voice in some decisions and make independent choices that will affect the journey.

There is one last section of the Project Overview form that you may wait to do: the row for checking what form the final reflection will take at the end of your project. If you want to plan that now, you may skip ahead to read about this step in the **Reflect and Perfect** chapter, pages 104 to 107, and make your decision. Or you may wait until you're in the middle of the project, since you might have a better sense then about how you want to handle the reflection process.

Ready, set, go — it's time to discuss how to manage your project in the next chapter.

Name of Project:		Duration:	
Subject/Course:		Grade Level:	
Other Subject Areas to Be Included:			

Project Idea Summary of the challenge, investigation, scenario, problem, or issue:	
Driving Question	
Content and Skills Standards to be addressed:	

21st Century Skills explicitly *taught and assessed* (T+A) or *encouraged* (E) by project work, but not taught or assessed:		T+A	E		T+A	E
	Collaboration	☐	☐	Other:	☐	☐
	Presentation	☐	☐		☐	☐
	Critical Thinking:	☐	☐		☐	☐

Culminating Products & Performances	Group:		**Presentation Audience:** ☐ Class ☐ School ☐ Community ☐ Experts ☐ Web ☐ Other:_____
	Individual:		

Entry Event to launch inquiry and engage students:		

Assessments	**Formative Assessments (During Project)**	Quizzes/Tests	☐	Practice Presentations	☐
		Journal/Learning Log	☐	Notes	☐
		Preliminary Plans/Outlines/Prototypes	☐	Checklists	☐
		Rough Drafts	☐	Concept Maps	☐
		Online Tests/Exams	☐		☐
	Summative Assessments (End of Project)	Written Product(s), with rubric: _____	☐	Other Product(s) or Performance(s), with rubric:_____	☐
		Oral Presentation, with rubric	☐	Peer Evaluation	☐
		Multiple Choice/Short Answer Test	☐	Self-Evaluation	☐
		Essay Test	☐	Other:	☐

Resources Needed	On-site people, facilities:	
	Equipment:	
	Materials:	
	Community resources:	

Reflection Methods	*(check all that will be used)*	Journal/Learning Log	☐	Focus Group	☐
		Whole-Class Discussion	☐	Fishbowl Discussion	☐
		Survey	☐	Other:	☐

Spotlight Project: *Projectile Motion*

PROJECT OVERVIEW page 1

Name of Project:	Projectile motion	Duration:	2 weeks
Subject/Course:	math (Algebra II/Trigonometry)	Grade Level:	11
Other Subject Areas to Be Included:	Physics		

Project Idea Summary of the challenge, investigation, scenario, problem, or issue:	Students work in teams to design and construct a ballistic device that launches an object in a flight path that follows a parabola. They use low cost materials (PVC pipe, plywood, rubber bands, etc.) to build the device, which must be capable of repeated firings. Students use knowledge of quadratic functions in order to hit a target. Each team conducts multiple tests and use the data they record to redesign their device if needed. Students make an oral presentation using PowerPoint slides to summarize their findings.

Driving Question	How can we build a device to launch a projectile, and calculate its motion in order to hit a target?

Content and Skills Standards to be addressed:

Students will be able to:
- use two-dimensional equations of motion for projectile motion to calculate initial velocity, time in the air, horizontal distance and maximum height.
- use trigonometry to resolve two-dimensional vectors into its vertical and horizontal components

- Graph quadratic equation and find x–intercepts, y–intercepts and vertex
- Apply factoring, quadratic formula and graphing calculator to find x–intercepts of a quadratic graph

<u>CA Content Standards</u> – Algebra II: 8.0, 10.0; Trigonometry: 12.0, 19.0; Physics: Ii, Ij

21st Century Skills explicitly *taught and assessed* (T+A) or *encouraged* (E) by project work, but not taught or assessed:

	T+A	E			T+A	E
Collaboration	☒	☐	Other: Critical and Creative Thinking; Problem Solving		☐	☒
Presentation	☒	☐			☐	☐
Critical Thinking:	☐	☐			☐	☐

Culminating Products & Performances

Group:	Design Proposal Complete Ballistic Device main Test Report	Angles of elevation Report Oral Presentation	**Presentation Audience:** ☒ Class ☒ School ☐ Community ☐ Experts ☐ Web ☐ Other:_____
Individual:	(no major individual products)		

Entry Event to launch inquiry and engage students:

Activity: Paper wad tossing contest (try to hit wastebasket, tossing over students of varying heights) and discussion of parabolas

Video: Scenes from last year's project (final tests of projectile launch devices)

Assessments

Formative Assessments (During Project)

[X] Quizzes/Tests	[X] Practice Presentations
[ ] Journal/Learning Log	[ ] Notes
[X] Preliminary Plans/Outlines/Prototypes	[ ] Checklists
[ ] Rough Drafts	[ ] Concept Maps
[ ] Online Tests/Exams	[ ] Other:

Summative Assessments (End of Project)

[ ] Written Product(s), with rubric: _____	[ ] Other Product(s) or Performance(s), with rubric: _____
[X] Oral Presentation, with rubric	[X] Peer Evaluation
[X] Multiple Choice/Short Answer Test	[X] Self-Evaluation
[ ] Essay Test	[ ] Other:

Resources Needed

On-site people, facilities: large open area for constructing and firing ballistic devices; other teachers and aides as available to help with construction

Equipment: measuring tape, LCD projector

Materials: low cost materials (PVC pipe, plywood, rubber bands, etc.) which may be provided or that students may collect

Community resources: none

Reflection Methods

(check all that will be used)

[ ] Journal/Learning Log	[ ] Focus Group
[ ] Whole-Class Discussion	[ ] Fishbowl Discussion
[X] Survey	[X] Other:

Spotlight Project: *Projectile Motion*

MANAGING YOUR PROJECT

This Chapter's Goal

All set? You've got your project idea, you've planned and prepared, and now it's ready for launch. In this chapter we'll help you effectively manage the implementation of your project by:

- Building a Culture of Inquiry and Independence

- Beginning the Inquiry Process After the Entry Event

- Managing Group Collaboration

- Keeping Track of Student Work

- Coaching the Inquiry Process

- Facilitating Presentations to an Audience

- Troubleshooting Common Problems

What Does Effective Project Management Look Like?

Before we start with the how-to, let's paint a picture of how it should look, ideally, when you and your students are actually working on a project. Of course, all projects are different, but think of the description below as a hazy vision of a perfect PBL classroom...

> *Students enter the classroom and know what they need to do. They gather in their groups and review their progress, the tasks to be done, the resources they need... and get to work. Students are asking questions. They are reading, writing, talking, using tools and equipment, calculating, making things, and going to their computers to conduct research, communicate, and create. The teacher moves among them, sometimes just listening, sometimes talking about their work process or about the content and skills students are learning. On other days, the teacher gives a lesson in response to students' questions about something they recognize they need to know, and students pay attention because they understand how it will help them complete project work. Curriculum resources and materials are available... the teacher is using formative assessments to check students' understanding of key facts and concepts... collaboration skills are practiced and documented. As the project reaches its climax, the energy level rises as students prepare for presentations and put final touches on the products they need to complete. The project culminates with well-paced, smoothly-delivered presentations to an engaged audience. Afterward, there is time for reflection and celebration.*

Nice vision, isn't it?

Not that *your* classroom will be any different from this vision, but *some* teachers might run into a few snags during a project. It happens to the best of them, because PBL is never completely predictable. This chapter will help you navigate the tricky waters between the launch of a project and the arrival at your destination: powerful learning for students, and the realization that they have done meaningful work.

A Word about Your Role as a PBL Teacher

During a project, you are still the content expert, as teachers are traditionally considered. But you are more than that. You are also a project co-manager, a facilitator, a coach, a cheerleader, and sometimes a counselor and higher authority if things get stressful or issues need to be resolved. The student-teacher relationship changes in PBL; it becomes closer, more personalized, more like colleagues on the job than an audience watching a "sage on the stage." If you're not already comfortable in these roles, you'll get used to it over time — or if you don't, you may decide that PBL is not for you.

Building a Culture of Inquiry and Independence

Know when to let go.

One of the hardest things for teachers to do during a project is to "let go" of their students. The traditional model of schooling involves a lot of spoon-feeding, hand-holding, and pouring-of-information-into-empty-heads. If this sounds anything like your classroom culture, it has to change in a PBL classroom. You may have to resist the urge to do things *for* students too quickly. Let them struggle a little — the right amount builds character.

When you planned your project, you set up many of the tasks students will accomplish and planned daily activities in ways that encouraged the two "I's" of inquiry and independence. Before the project started, you built students' skills to help them be able to work in this way. Now that the project is rolling along, it's important to continue nurturing that "positive I and I vibration," as they might say at a reggae concert.

You nurture the spirit of inquiry and independence to a great extent by the way you act in the classroom, when you model the behaviors and attitudes you want to promote. You know the sayings: Practice what you preach, children learn what they live, monkey see monkey do. It may not always be easy, since the behaviors might be new to you, so you might catch yourself modeling "old school" ways of acting and thinking on occasion. If that happens, you could make it a teachable moment — stop and point out to your students that "we're all new to PBL" and making mistakes shows that we're learning.

> **TIPS FROM THE CLASSROOM**
>
> ## Give Students the (Pointer) Finger
>
> After you launch your project, you'll likely get the standard array of questions from students about due dates, points, does spelling and grammar count, how many pages does it have to be, and so on. Do not answer these questions right away, because answering every time they're asked (and they will be repeated) does not nurture a culture of independence. Instead, point to where students can find the answers themselves, such as a packet of materials available in a Project Center, file drawer, or online if you've gone high-tech.

Establishing the right classroom culture for a project

The culture of a classroom is shaped by how you as the teacher behave. Here are some do's and don'ts.

Do	Don't
Allow students to voice their opinions, contribute ideas, and ask questions freely.	*Appear* to welcome the ideas of students, but then do it your way anyway.
Teach students how to offer constructive, diplomatic critique of each other's ideas and work.	Say, "there are no dumb questions," then roll your eyes when one is asked.
	Allow students to criticize each others' questions, comments and work in a hurtful way.
Encourage creative thinking and problem-solving behaviors such as brainstorming and trial-and-error.	Try to steer students along a path that limits their own ideas, or leads them toward a solution or answer *you* think is best.
Allow students to make suggestions about the project and make choices about how to do things, given what is realistic and practical.	Tell students they can't do something "because I'm the boss" or without carefully leading them to see *why* they can't do it.
Let students know that it's OK to make a mistake, "because that's how learning works. That's how we need to approach our job in a project like this."	Penalize students for mistakes made during practice presentations or on rough drafts, mock-ups, storyboards, etc.
	Express your disappointment or disapproval when students offer an idea or solution to a problem that you think is off-target.
Try to make your first response, "How could you find that out?" when a student asks a question.	Say, "That's a good question. Let me give you a lecture about that," before students have had chance to investigate for themselves.
Let students find websites, books, articles, and other sources of information on their own as much as possible.	Hand students a list of required websites and highlighted articles and summaries of books that you've assembled all weekend.
Create a list of expectations with students for how they should work during the project. Post this list in the classroom, revisiting and revising with students when necessary.	Assume students know how they should work during the project, because you've explained it over and over, or because "it should be obvious."

Beginning the Inquiry Process
after the Entry Event

Bon Voyage!

Remember what we said in the last chapter when you were planning how to begin your project. The first phase of the project launch is an Entry Event that:

- Generates student interest.

- Takes place on Day One of your Project Calendar.

- Should NOT be preceded by teaching students what they will need to know in terms of project-specific content knowledge.

- Should NOT be preceded or accompanied immediately by a detailed description of the project — or by an intimidating load of paper dumped on students' desks. Allow students to get engaged before concerns start to arise.

Although there are many possible kinds of Entry Events, after it occurs you need to start students on the path toward completion of the project.

Project Launch, Phase Two: I've Got Their Attention, Now What?

The basic goals of the second phase of the Project Launch are to generate student questions and ideas, familiarize students with the requirements of the project, and then have them get to work. Although the time for the second phase of the Project Launch may vary — it typically takes from one to two class periods — the steps after the Entry Event are the same for any project:

1. **Present students with the Driving Question** and let them discuss it, wonder and share thoughts about it, and perhaps brainstorm additional sub-questions that explore various aspects of it. (Note: Eventually you can have students help create a Driving Question for some projects, but wait until you've become a more accomplished PBL teacher.)

2. **Analyze the task(s) required in the project**. Tell students about the culminating products and presentations, if your Entry Event did not make it clear. Ask students to identify exactly what they need to do to reach that goal, and identify the skills and knowledge they will we need. (See below for details on how to conduct this discussion.)

Tell Students When They Will Present

Be wary of negotiating presentation schedules with students. As you might expect, they tend toward "as far away as possible." It's better to make the presentation schedule a done deal that you announce on the day the project launches.

3. **Identify resources** that might help students gain the skills and knowledge they need—ask students to contribute ideas, but also tell them what they can expect to be provided by you.

4. **Explain some of the details**, either orally or on a handout, including:

   ▸ Showing students the Project Calendar with due dates, checkpoints, and major events

   ▸ Making sure students understand the rubric(s) and other assessment and grading details, including how much the project "counts"

   ▸ Letting students know who they will be working with

   ▸ Explaining how project work will be organized, such as where to find and keep important items (either online or in a special place in the classroom) and how daily and weekly work will be monitored

5. **Have students meet in their groups**, to start working on tasks such as:

   ▸ Doing a team-builder or icebreaker activity (sharing what each member is good at might be helpful)

   ▸ Discussing and completing their Group Contract or other set of expectations and commitments

   ▸ Brainstorming a list of ideas and/or creating a concept map about the topic, task, and/or Driving Question (this can help students see alternate approaches, secondary questions, or connections between topics)

   ▸ Begin managing their project work by creating an initial list of tasks to be done, by whom, by when, and an initial plan for gathering resources and doing research

✻ USE THIS SAMPLE PROJECT GROUP CONTRACT (*page 129*)

PROJECT MANAGEMENT LOG:
GROUP TASKS (*page 126*)

How to conduct a "need to know" discussion

Creating a "need to know" list is one example of a structured process for analyzing the tasks required in the project, as described in Step 2 above. The list helps students get organized at the start of a project, and also can be used to check progress along the way.

1. After making sure students understand what the project requires, ask them to think about what they would need to know, in order to successfully complete the task they have been given.

   Tip: *If you think students may need help getting started—or you are met with blank looks—have them generate some items for the list by talking with a partner or in small groups. You also could model the process with some examples, since students may be new to this kind of thinking.*

2. On a flipchart, the board, or a computer projector so everyone can see, write the words, "What Do We Need to Know?" Remember that each class doing the project will need to record and preserve its own distinct list.

   Tip: *Ask for a volunteer to be a recorder. This frees you to facilitate the discussion.*

3. Record all ideas and questions on the appropriate chart/column, capturing students' exact words.

   Tip: *Do not try to edit or reshape students' questions and comments, or it will feel like you're making the words yours when they should be "owned" by students, in a culture of inquiry and independence.*

4. Do not attempt to answer questions yet.

   Tip: *Resist the urge, although this may seem counterintuitive and certainly flies in the face of traditional teaching practice. Remember that culture of independence.*

Bulletin Board

A "Need to Know" List Created After the Entry Event for "A Balancing Act"

Here's a sample of what Jennifer's class listed after her students received the memo asking them to design an ecosystem for a biosphere in a reality TV show:

What Do We Need to Know?

- *What does self-sustaining mean?*
- *Which ecosystem do we get?*
- *What's a biome?*
- *What's tundra and a coniferous and deciduous forest?*
- *What is a biological community?*
- *How should we make our drawings?*
- *What should be in our report?*

5. Prompt students to add to the list if you notice they are not identifying "need to knows" that you know they will need, especially if it relates to key content knowledge which students may not gravitate toward.

   Tip: *Do this subtly, like Socrates would have done. Ask, "How about this part of the project—what would you need to learn to be able to do that?" or "Do you understand what this means?"*

6. Keep the "need to know" list on display and revisit it from time to time as a management tool during the project. Check items off the list as they become "known" and add new items as they emerge.

   Tip: *When you introduce a lesson or provide a resource to students, point to the need to know list to remind students that they identified it as something that will help them with their project. This helps students see the context and feel like their voice has been heard—and pay closer attention!*

Managing Group Collaboration

Keep that machine well-oiled.

You formed student groups before the project was launched. This saved a great deal of time, since were able to think carefully about how to compose teams before students bombarded you with questions, concerns, and pleas at the beginning of the project. However, the fact that you designed the groups doesn't mean they will work together effectively. It's often hard enough for adults in the workplace to function well as a team. And you know your students—raging hormones, still-developing social skills, and who knows what baggage from their lives outside of your classroom—so working in groups might be hard for them. You're probably going to need to build their collaboration skills before and during a project, as we noted in the **Planning and Preparing** chapter. And you'll need to monitor their group interaction, intervening if necessary.

At the start of a project...

To help student groups get smoothly underway and hold them accountable:

- Discuss with the whole class what it means to "work effectively as a team." Ask students to describe what you would see and hear when this is happening. Construct a list and keep it posted. (These are sometimes called "ground rules," "norms," or "expectations.")

- Building from the discussion described above, show students a rubric for collaboration skills (in future projects, you may have them help write one as a class exercise).

■ Have students sign a "contract" that specifies what is expected of all group members. You can provide one for them, like the one in the back of this book, or they could create their own.

■ Provide a "Task List" or "Project Work Plan" template, to help students organize themselves. You can use the *Project Management Log* in the back of this book.

■ Give students clear directions for an initial brainstorming session. Ask them to turn in written evidence of what they have done, such as a list of questions and ideas, or a diagram with words in circles connected by lines that show how concepts or steps in a process are related.

COLLABORATION RUBRIC (*page 124*)   **✱USE THIS**

PROJECT GROUP CONTRACT (*page 129*)

PROJECT MANAGEMENT LOG:
GROUP TASKS (*page 126*)

PROJECT WORK REPORT: INDIVIDUAL (*page 127*)

PROJECT WORK REPORT: GROUP (*page 128*)

In the midst of a project...

To monitor their progress, collaboration skills, and to help student groups keep working smoothly:

■ On a regular basis, have students report on how well they are getting tasks done. This could be daily — if you think they need close attention — or every other day, or even weekly if things are going well. A whole-class discussion might help you gauge how well things are going generally, but you'll also need specific information from each student and/or group. Go around the room and meet with each group, and/or collect something in writing from each group or each student.

When Students Come and Go

Some teachers work in fluid environments in which there is a rapid turnover of students. Even in more stable situations, students will sometimes get sick or go on a trip and miss project work time. You may need to decide on a case-by-case basis, but here are some questions to ask yourself, with a few thoughts from experienced PBL teachers:

What will I do if new students enter my classroom mid-project?

- Put them in a group that you think will be most accepting.

- It depends on the project, but somewhere around the mid-point is usually too late for a new student to join a group; let him or her help out, but not bear much responsibility. Provide an alternative way to learn the content knowledge.

What will I do if students leave my classroom for an extended time?

- Ask the students who left to do the project individually, perhaps with fewer requirements.

- Depending on how many members are lost, ask the group to make do with fewer members, even if it's a pair.

- If a group loses too many members, let the remaining students join another group.

- Offer more time and/or extra credit to the remaining group members if they suddenly have a great deal of work to do.

- At checkpoints on your Project Calendar, or whenever you think they need it, have groups pause to discuss how well they are working together. Have them refer to the collaboration rubric or list of ground rules, and hand in a short report or checklist evaluating themselves.

  ▶ In addition to general monitoring by walking around to watch and listen, sit with and observe each group at least twice per project and provide them with feedback.

  ▶ Hold a meeting of team leaders at least once during a project, or more often if it seems necessary. Ask them to report how well things are going and let you know if any problems are arising.

  ▶ Intervene with any group that appears to have serious conflicts or logjams. Pull them aside for a conference and try to help them through the situation — as much as possible by asking *them* to come up with possible solutions rather than dictating what they should do. (If a group is *really* dysfunctional, see *Troubleshooting Tips* below).

Bulletin Board

Helicopters and Predator Drones: Your Style for Monitoring Groups

There are two distinct styles of managing groups in a PBL classroom. Some teachers literally hover over student groups to ensure they stay on task at all times. These micromanagers are reluctant to relinquish control. Let's call them helicopters. Other teachers stay near the front of the room or move around the periphery, using their eyes and ears to monitor noise, motion and work. They are Predator Drones. They can zoom in when needed or fire a verbal missile from across the room to quell a disturbance. These teachers are in total command of their room, but not total control of every action in every group.

Hard-learned classroom experience shows that the Predator Drone method is more effective in a PBL environment. In most instances, it's best to let groups work independently. After all, you're trying to encourage critical thinking, collaboration and communication. If you maintain too much control of your groups you limit the opportunities students have to practice and develop these skills. If your students are new to PBL you may have to "hover" more often, but you'll be able to pull back as they get more experienced.

No, you can't use a dumpster.

As soon as your project is launched, the papers should begin to arrive, like the first flurries of a blizzard. On the first or second day, at a minimum you should receive a copy of each group's contract and their first task list (they keep a copy too). Early in a project, many PBL teachers require their groups to submit brainstorming notes and sketches, concept maps, and time logs. You never know which document or artifact might play a crucial role in telling the story of how a group did their work on a project, so capture the process by using paper folders or setting up an online system.

It's a good idea to keep work products in the classroom or on a central online location, because it's easy for a project to get derailed by absent students who have the only copy of a group's resource list, interview notes, rough draft, or presentation materials. Remember, you're trying to teach 21st century skills and effective work habits in PBL. In the business world when the boss asks to see what you've produced, it just won't cut it to say, "My buddy's got it in his locker but he's on a field trip... for three days."

Here are tips from some oh-so-organized PBL teachers about how to keep track of project work:

Online:

- On your school-provided website or your own, create project pages containing key documents and places to store student work. Create a blog to communicate with students about the project.

- Set up a wiki for the project, so students can share information, resources, and post their work for collaborative input.

- Use a Web-based "desktop" application such as Drupal (**http://drupal. org**) and Textpattern (**http://textpattern.com**) that provides content management and blogging features and other systems for online discussions and collaborative student work.

Hard copy:

- Get some Manila folders, one for each group, and label it with everyone's name, class period, project name, etc.

- On the inside cover, write or attach key project information like due dates, calendar, points possible, etc.

- Store the folders in a special place on your desk, a filing cabinet, or a "Project Center" part of your classroom.

- Use a checkout form when each group uses the folder each day in class; the folder must be returned and signed in at the end of the class period.

Bulletin Board A Good Book About Technology in PBL

For lots of great ideas (like the ones on page 90) about how to use technology to manage your project, as well as useful advice on how to design technology-rich projects, check out:

Reinventing Project Based Learning:
Your Field Guide to Real-World Projects in the Digital Age

By Suzie Boss and Jane Krauss

Published by International Society for Technology in Education, 2007
http://www.iste.org/source/orders/isteproduct
detail.cfm?product_code=reinvt

Coaching the Inquiry Process

Getting students to dig deeper.

At some point mid-way through your project, you might notice that your students are not, well, *thinking* very hard. They're getting tasks done, producing work, not goofing off... but it all feels vaguely perfunctory, too superficial, like it's missing that intellectual spark-fest you imagined when you first envisioned your project. You wonder, Is it them? Is it me? Is it my project? Well, the answer is potentially "all of the above." But take heart — it might be fixable! Or at least understandable, and a lesson learned for your next project.

If you find yourself in this situation, here are some questions to ask yourself, followed by our suggestions:

- Is this the first time students have been asked to think this way, and/or do they need to be shown what it looks like?

  Pull the whole class together and model what it looks like when you "dig deep" into a topic. Use a challenging piece of reading, an application of a mathematical concept, a finding from an experiment or survey, or the Driving Question itself, and "think aloud" about further questions that could be raised, where an investigation might lead, and what resources might be helpful in exploring the topic further. Encourage students to think aloud as well. You could also give them a list of prompts that direct their thinking to specific questions or topics.

- Are students turning to you for answers to their questions, instead of finding their own answers?

  *Hold back and allow more time for students to develop their own answers to questions. Say, "I don't know — how could you find that out?" You could also encourage an independent inquiry process by having students and groups be responsible for different questions and share information or resources with each other, a.k.a. the "jigsaw" technique (for more information see **www.jigsaw.org**).*

- If students will be assessed according to how well they display "critical thinking skills," are they well aware of this and do they know what it means?

  Remind students that their major products and performances require a demonstration of critical thinking, which will be assessed using a rubric that describes it (if this is in fact true). Show them examples of work that shows clear evidence of what is described in the rubric. Go one step further, and have them practice using the rubric by critiquing multiple examples of work.

- Do the tasks and products you have asked students to complete really require them to dig deep? Or is your Driving Question too simple?

  Help students make the connection between the Driving Question and project tasks if it's not readily apparent. You could assign some additional "deep" questions to answer in a presentation or in written work, as long as it does not appear to be an unfair increase in the workload or a sudden shift in the task.

Facilitating Presentations to an Audience

Time to shine.

On most days during a project you'll probably find yourself relatively relaxed, because it's much easier to teach on a daily basis in a PBL classroom when you've corralled all your resources and completed your planning before the project was launched. But near the end, if your students are presenting to someone other than you and their classmates, your heart rate might speed up a bit. When the kids brush teeth, put on their Sunday best — or at least tuck in their shirts and pull up their pants — and fire up those LCD projectors, they're not the only nervous people in the room. After all, it's your work on display, too. Here's how to make the day go as smoothly as possible.

Before Presentation Day: Be Prepared

If you planned your project thoroughly and arranged your resources before it started, the logistics — schedule, facilities, equipment, and personnel — should not be an issue on presentation day. But just to help make sure you've got everything ready, we've provided a checklist in the back of this book.

On Presentation Day: How to Wear Two Hats

Hat #1: Host With the Most

Wear this hat if any guests are coming into your classroom, and especially when community members or parents are visiting the school. You'll need to put on your meet-and-greet face to welcome them, making sure they know where to sit and where the refreshments and restrooms are.

Inform your audience about what they should do:

- If the audience is going to be passive — simply watching and listening but not asking probing questions or evaluating the presenters — just tell them what to expect, whether they should ask questions, and when to break into wild applause.

- If presentations are to be kept to a strict time limit, let the presenters and audience know that you might be giving signals to wrap it up or cut short a question session.

- If you think a student audience needs a reminder about "how to be a good audience," give it.

- If the audience is playing a more active, complex role for which they have been prepared, give them just a quick reminder.

You may want to give your audience some handouts:

- a written summary of the project

- a list of sample questions to ask (about both content and process, if you wish)

- a form for recording their feedback and comments

TIPS FROM THE CLASSROOM

Prepare Your Audience for Complex Duties

If the audience or panel members for presentations will be play-acting a role that will be somewhat demanding, explain it to them thoroughly. If they are acting as active assessors of student work, they'll also need advance preparation. Send key documents and coach them via phone calls, email, online postings, or perhaps by meeting with them. If they're going to be using a checklist or a rubric, it definitely would be best to meet with them ahead of time to explain how to use it — but beware, a rubric may be too complex a tool for an "amateur" to operate safely!

Hat #2: Keen-Eyed, Sharp-Eared Assessor

Wear this hat once the presentations begin. Put your rubric(s) in front of you, make sure you can see and hear well, then get ready to pay close attention. If you're making a video recording of the presentations, you can refer to it later to help you remember and assess, but that takes time. Get as much done as you can during the live action.

Ideally, you should assess your students while observing and listening as *other* people ask questions and probe their understanding and knowledge. If others are asking questions, even stock questions you provided, you are free to focus 100% of your attention on what your students say and do. If you are the only one with the expertise to ask certain questions, you may need to join in, but try to step back and watch as much as possible.

Here are some suggestions for asking questions following a presentation:

If you want to find out if students really **understand a concept**, or whether they have just memorized some words to say...

Ask questions such as:

Can you restate that in other words?

Could you give me an analogy for that?

Can you explain that in another way?

If you want to find out **students' depth and breadth of knowledge** of a topic...

Ask questions such as:

Would you explain that in more detail?

Can you give me some more facts about that?

Could you give me more examples?

Can you tell me more about the context of that?

If you want to find out if students can **correctly use new or technical vocabulary...**

Ask questions such as:

Could you define that for me?

Can you tell me what that means?

If you want to find out if students can **think critically**, recognize implications, and make connections from their topic to other issues, applications, and possibilities — basically to "see the big picture"...

Ask questions such as:

Could you connect that with ____?

Can you imagine how that might ____?

How might someone look at this from the perspective of ____?

How would someone react to ____ if they were ____?

What other possibilities could you see for ____?

Can you tell me how that might apply to ____?

What issues might this bring up for ____?

What else might be affected by ____?

If you want to find out **how and why students did what they did** in the project...

Ask questions such as:

Could you tell me how you found that information?

How did you reach that conclusion or find that solution?

What alternatives did you consider and why?

What evidence did you feel was strongest and why?

What challenges did you overcome?

What questions do you have that are still unanswered or require further information?

Keep the Other Students Busy While a Group is Presenting.

Another common question in PBL is, "What do I do with the rest of the class during presentations?"

Here are some ideas:

- Teach students how to be a good audience, then remind them. Repeat as necessary.

- Give them a task, such as taking notes on key points or strong arguments; writing down questions to ask afterward; scoring each other on a rubric or checklist.

- If you have reasons for not wanting students to see another group's presentation beforehand, arrange to put them in two separate rooms, if possible. Once students present, they can become audience members for groups that follow.

Questioning Individual Students after a Group Presentation

To help you assess individual learning in PBL, you need to ask questions when students present as a group. But students can be slippery characters, especially when it comes to standing up in front of an audience to display what they know and can do. It's a scary time, even for many adults (after all, doesn't "speaking in public" rank just above "death" on lists of what people fear most?). When students are making a presentation as a member of a group, you've probably seen and heard many of what psychologists call *avoidance behaviors*:

> *"I'm the one who holds up the poster (in front of my face)."*

> *"I only introduce the other members and tell what they're going to explain."*

> *"I made the PowerPoint slides so I don't have to talk."*

> *"We each learned only our part of the presentation so I'm just reading off my note cards and please don't ask me any questions about anything else. I have no idea what my teammates are talking about."*

You may have found ways to prevent the avoidance behaviors back when you designed your project and told students that everyone must deliver a substantive part of the presentation. And perhaps you're handling the individual assessment issue by collecting some written work from each student and also by giving a test. However, perhaps you do want to gather some data during a presentation on what each member of the group may have learned. Give students fair warning ahead of time, then try these tricks from the masters:

- Have each student individually answer at least two questions about his or her work, with no help from teammates.

- Ask a student to answer a question about what another student has presented.

- If you want to be "extra rigorous" (or, some might say, "mean"), tell students that you may call on *any* one of them to deliver *any* part of the presentation, so they *all* had better know it well.

Troubleshooting Common Problems

Just when you thought it was going so well.

Cut yourself some slack. Your first project is not going to go perfectly, and neither will your second. Learning to live with a certain amount of "messiness" is part of PBL. But unless things really fall apart, DO NOT cancel a project entirely once it has begun. This sends the message to students that when things get tough, the not-so-tough bail out instead of finding ways to make the effort worthwhile. Instead, you might want to call a time out to discuss the project with students — find out what's going on, and problem-solve together. You also could ask a colleague for suggestions, consult with organizations or other people with expertise, or try the ideas below.

How to Deal with Common Problems

If the project is taking too long

You can try this:
- Reduce the scope of the work by cutting back on the number, length or complexity of student products. *Example:* A formal oral presentation by each group becomes a "fishbowl" discussion in front of the class among representatives of each group.

- Schedule more guided instruction. *Example:* Step-by-step teacher-led walkthrough of how to write a persuasive essay.

- Allow students or groups to complete some tasks collectively. *Example:* Shared bibliography or PowerPoint template.

If the project doesn't take as long as you anticipated

You can try this:

- Finish early. Remember, no one gets the length of the project just right the first time they run it. Take notes and make improvements for the second time you'll run the project.

- Use multiple evaluations. *Example:* Students or groups who finish work early must undergo one or more peer assessments using the rubrics you created for the project.

- Turn students loose. *Example:* Meet with the fast workers and brainstorm extensions of project work they can create on their own.

If the outside resources or people are not available

You can try this:

- Create problem solvers. *Example:* Students use problem-solving skills to create a backup plan in case resources are lost or unavailable.

- Turn to technology. *Examples:* Virtual tours using online resources; Find and show video that provides information about the project; Conduct and record phone interviews with project resources; Have students create interview questions and email those to outside experts.

If the student groups aren't working well together

You can try this:

- Re-establish collaboration skills. *Example:* Teacher acts as facilitator and engages problematic groups in skill building activities, such as those described in the *If and How to Prepare Students for PBL* section of the **Planning and Preparing** chapter.

- Seek help. *Example:* Bring in a counselor or outside facilitator who specializes in conflict resolution (Note: Every teacher's union and district office has one or more of these folks).

- Become the project manager. *Example:* With problematic groups, the teacher steps in to control the workflow and interaction.

- Last resort: break up the group and scatter members among other groups, or have individuals or pairs complete the project on their own.

If you don't have time to give feedback

You can try this:

- Check a sample, not the entire class. Be sure to check a range of samples you suspect will be of high, medium, and low quality.

- Have students assess themselves and/or each other, then report results to you. Use this data to plan interventions or additional instruction as needed.

- Assign groups or individuals different due dates for longer pieces of work, such as rough drafts of research papers, so you're not trying to read 30 papers at once. Or, tell students they may turn in rough drafts anytime within a certain period, not just on one day.

If you realize the Driving Question is too big

You can try this:

- Discuss and reflect. *Example:* Ask students to reflect mid-project on their grasp of the Driving Question and use those reflections to rewrite the DQ so it's more kid-friendly.

- Create sub-questions during the Planning and Preparing phase, or invent some quickly now, that relate to various aspects of the Driving Question. Redirect project focus to these more achievable sub-questions.

If students can't find information or can't sort through a large quantity of information

You can try this:

- Provide the resources. *Example:* Teacher finds websites, brings in books from the library, or photocopies research material.

- Reduce the scope of the research. *Example:* Require only 2 book citations instead of 5, and only 3 web citations instead of 10.

- Provide a lesson on how to find the most useful information. *Examples:* Show students how to use the right words to focus a web search, and how to think about what sites might be more or less credible; Display a website, show how to navigate through it, and check for point of view and accuracy.

If the project products are too difficult and/or time-consuming

You can try this:

- Hold meetings with groups and discuss how to set a timeline and accomplish tasks efficiently.

- Reduce scope of work. *Examples:* Reduce PSA from a produced video to a detailed storyboard; Change working model to scale model or 3-D rendering.

If students have not learned some material well enough

You can try this:

- Make sure to allow enough time after the presentations are over to review important content with students.

- Add a test, essay or other assignment (but give students enough time to prepare, so it seems fair)

- If only some students among the class have not learned well enough, have them complete an additional assignment, re-do a culminating product, or retake the test.

- Re-teach some material after the project if it is important enough, either through direct instruction or by including it in a future unit or project.

REFLECT AND PERFECT

This Chapter's Goal

Whew. Almost there—time for the last phase of your project, after the presentations are over and culminating products have been collected. In this chapter we'll explain how to reflect upon and improve your project by:

- Celebrating Success

- Facilitating Student Reflection about What They Have Learned

- Guiding Students in Self and Group Assessment

- Using Data to Plan Future Action and Improve Your Project

- Gathering Feedback from Students about the Design and Management of the Project

- Collecting Your Thoughts about How the Project Went

- Collecting and Saving Examples of Student Work

Why "Reflect" After a Project Ends?

Taking the time to reflect on a project is an important last step that often gets overlooked. It's not about admiring yourself in the mirror. Research shows that reflection helps students retain what they learn, and it can help you improve your project and plan for the next one. So even if after the big finish you'd just like to relax and show a video, allow yourself and your students some time to think about what you've been through.

The last step of a project is also a good time to ask students to assess the collaboration skills of themselves and their peers, as they reflect on the process they used to learn and complete tasks.

There's another reason to include time to reflect on your project calendar. It has to do with what psychologists would call the "affective domain"—in other words, the emotional side of PBL. Not to get all touchy-feely here, but after a lengthy, challenging, and (you hope) rewarding and exciting experience together, a group should recognize the significance of what it has accomplished. If your project ended with whiz-bang presentations to an audience on Friday, wouldn't it somehow feel *wrong* on Monday to just move on to the next unit without a look back? That's what usually happens in school, after the "Friday test." A project should strike students as being different from traditional instruction. So use thoughtful reflection time to drive home that realization—and make them look forward to their next project!

> A group should recognize the significance of what it has accomplished.

Celebrating Success

How about a group hug!

Before you ask students to work some more—which is what it will feel like when you ask for evaluation and reflection—take a moment to celebrate at the end of the project. It helps show that PBL mirrors life in the workplace.

Almost everyone celebrates the completion of good work. Office workers go out to dinner, politicians cut ceremonial ribbons, nurses and doctors hug patients and salespeople high-five their boss. Sports provide lots of examples, such as when athletes parade down Main Street and trophies are awarded. The completion of a project in a classroom should be no different—except maybe not with the showoff dance moves in the end zone or Gatorade poured on the coach.

The celebration can be formal or informal. Here are some ideas.

Ways to Celebrate a Project:

- Invite audience members to stay around after presentations for a reception, to talk informally with students and offer praise.

- Invite school and/or district administrators who were aware of the project, or outside experts, community members and parents who were involved, to visit your classroom and offer congratulations.

- In a whole-class activity, tell your students how proud you are, with specific examples. Then ask them to add more ideas to a list of "What We Are Proud Of."

- Let your community know. Get a local reporter for a newspaper, radio or TV station to cover your project and tout the results. Arrange for project work to be displayed at a local government office, business, public library, museum, gallery, community center, etc.

- Conduct an "awards ceremony," but be careful not to make the "losers" feel like losers even though they worked hard. You could give a variety of awards, which could be serious ("Best Solution," "Most Creative Solution," or "Hardest Working") or not so serious ("Best Dressed for Presentations," "Least Number of Times the Teacher Was Asked 'Can We Have Another Copy of That Handout We Lost?'" or "Future Dot-Com Entrepreneurs, for Best Use of Technology").

- Create an archive or "memorial" of some kind. Students could create a display of their work, contribute words or phrases to a signed "This Project Was..." poster to go on the classroom wall, assemble images and writing in a scrapbook, or place project artifacts in online archive. These memorials could be kept with pride all year, shown to parents, visitors, administrators and colleagues, and to other students as helpful examples of what good PBL looks like.

> Almost everyone celebrates the completion of good work... the completion of a project should be no different

Facilitating Student Reflection About Learning

Take a look in the rearview mirror.

As soon as possible after the project's culminating presentations, after all the products have been turned in and (if applicable) the tests taken, ask your students to look back on the journey they've completed. But before you decide on *what* to ask them, decide *how* you want them to respond. We recommend a combination of individual, small group, and whole-class methods.

How students can reflect on a project

- Individual journal entry, a set of written responses, or a survey

---

✻ USE THIS   SELF-REFLECTION ON PROJECT WORK FORM (*page 132*)

TIPS FROM THE **CLASSROOM**

Polish Up that Reflectivity

Students may not see the value of reflection, and many will tend to answer questions quickly and without much thought. To counteract this tendency, here are three ideas:

- Jump-start the process by having students discuss the project with a partner or in small groups, then write individual reflections

- Provide an example of what a thoughtful comment looks like

- Assign points or a grade to increase motivation to do a good job

- Think-Pair-Share, in which individuals jot down a response, share it with a partner, then contribute to a whole-class discussion. Record comments for everyone to see. (See the table below for questions to ask about the project's content and process.)

- Small group discussion, followed by whole-class. Record comments for everyone to see.

- Fishbowl discussion, in which each group sends a representative to the front of the room to sit in a circle to discuss the project as the class listens. You can leave an "open chair" for any class member to pop in with a comment. Record comments for everyone to see.

What students can reflect and report on

The Content:

- What did we learn?
  (It's OK to start with a general question like this, but then quickly move to specifics)

- What is your answer to the Driving Question now? How did your thinking about it change during the project?

- What other topics does this project make you wonder about? What other relevant questions could be investigated, or other problems addressed?

- What is the best solution to the problem and why? What other solutions might make sense?

- How did skills and knowledge from other school subjects help answer the Driving Question, or help you do the work you needed to do?

- What skills did you learn in the project that relate to a particular subject in school? (e.g., writing, calculating, doing an experiment, creating an artifact)

The Process:

- Did we/you collaborate effectively? What would have made us better collaborators?

- Did we/you use effective presentation skills? How could we have improved?

- Did we/you use effective problem-solving skills? If things went wrong, what happened?

- Did we/you use effective time management and work organization skills? What would you do differently next time?

- How good was the quality of our work? Where can we improve?

- What skills do we/you need to practice some more?

Take that Last Chance to Correct Misunderstandings

When students offer comments on what they have learned, you may notice that they still don't quite understand a concept or a process clearly. Maybe they're slightly misusing a key term, or not seeing the connection between what they learned and its application to something else. You might have picked up on this misunderstanding during presentations too, despite your best efforts to catch it in advance by providing formative feedback, checking rough drafts, and watching practice presentations. And it may have been glaringly obvious from your assessment of their work or test results that students simply didn't fully "get" something important.

If this happens, take the time while the moment is ripe to clarify their thinking. If it's only a few students, you could talk with them separately, but if it's many, act now with the whole class. Even if it means taking more time than you planned, this is one of those "teachable moments" when students are most ready to learn. Don't let them walk out the door as you slap your head and say "doh!"

Guiding Students in Self and Group Assessment

It's NOT snitching, it's "peer evaluation."

By the time your project ends, students should know more about what 21st century skills like collaboration and communication look like in practice. Students will have used these skills during the project, and they will have seen rubrics for them and thought about them at various checkpoints you established. So when you ask students to use a rubric *and* provide evidence for their scores, you can collect some valuable data to add to your own evaluation.

However, when it comes time to ask students to evaluate themselves and their peers on their collaboration skills, a funny thing may happen. They may say one of two things:

> *"I was a great team member and our whole group worked really well together!"*
>
> *or*
>
> *"I was a great team member but some others I'd rather not name could have done more."*

It's human nature to want to put yourself in the best possible light. And it's definitely the nature of many middle and high school students to adhere to a code of honor that prohibits them from getting too specific about who did the heavy lifting in a group and who freeloaded. Of course, this depends on the individual student, and on your classroom culture — and the more projects you do, the more students will tend to be honest as they get used to the process, and both they and you get serious about the norm, "everyone contributes, no one slides by."

Encouraging students to report accurately

- Explain to students that they will need to provide specific evidence to back up an assessment of their own and their peers' work. It will not be enough to say, "I give myself an 'A'!" — they need to point out exactly what they did, when, how, and so on.

- Remind students that their assessment of themselves will be checked against what other group members say and by your own observations and assessment of their work. Major differences may be discussed in a private conference with the teacher, but you will have the final say.

- Have each student anonymously use the collaboration rubric to assess other members of the group. Average the scores to assign a grade or points for each student, protecting the source of each individual score.

- Give each group 100 points to divide among themselves, based on how much each member contributed to the effort. Ask them to write down specific evidence to support their scores, and see if this matches your observations. If it doesn't, adjust the points — and let students know ahead of time that you might do this.

Using Data to Plan Future Action and Improve Your Project

Sure, it was fun, but what did they learn?

We've said it before — a project is a journey that can be exciting, challenging, rewarding, and downright fun. But when the journey ends, after all the looking back and thoughtful comments and celebration, remember to ask the BIG question: Did we get where we intended to go? You specified several goals when you designed the project, so use the data you've collected to analyze the results of your project with a clear, unblinking eye.

Sources of data about student achievement in a project:

- Your own observations as students worked

- Your analysis of culminating products and performances, including how they compare to previous work your students have done

- Comments from other adults who served as resources or mentors, or who saw culminating products and performances

- Scores from assessment rubrics

- Tests and quizzes

- Students' self-reports and reflections

- Standardized tests or other assessments not created by you

What to do if the data reveal a shortfall:

1. Make note of which standards (knowledge, understanding, and skills) were not learned well enough.

2. Decide if the standards should be re-taught immediately, using other methods besides PBL, or whether they could be included in a future project.

3. Make note of which 21st century skills, or which aspects of them, were not being used effectively.

4. Decide if, when, and how certain 21st century skills should be emphasized in future projects.

5. Start thinking about how you could reinforce the teaching of the standards and other skills the next time you run the same project.

Gathering Feedback from Students about Project Design and Management

Tell me the truth, I can handle it.

After a project ends you probably will have a sense of its strengths and weaknesses, but be sure to also ask your students for their thoughts. This is a good idea for two reasons. First, students might have experienced things or have a point of view that you did not see or realize. Second, students' opinions should matter in PBL — they were not just passive recipients of your teaching, but active partners on the journey. In other words, they *deserve* a chance to contribute ideas for improving the project. Oh, there's a third reason you might need to remember especially if your project did not go as well as you hoped: students might point out some good things that happened, and save you from that nagging "Why did I do all this?" feeling.

As we said above, first you need to decide how you want to gather feedback from students. It could be through a survey, a journal, or a discussion.

What You Could Ask Students about a Project's Design and Management:

- Was it the right length of time?

- How was the workload (including the complexity and frequency of the assignments)?

- Were the instructions clear?

Next Summer, Remember What You Did

Few teachers have the time to make improvements in the design of their project during the school year. Save that work for the dog days of summer, but in the near term create a folder labeled "Project Improvements" and file named for each project you run. Use this to store student feedback, record your own notes, and add any new ideas or resources you gather.

- Were the assessments fair?

- Were the resources you needed available?

- Did you get the right amount of help from me/the teacher, but not too much control?

- Was the project interesting, challenging in a good way, fun?

- What were the biggest challenges?

- Do you have any other ideas for how the project could be improved?

Collecting Your Thoughts about How the Project Went

Can't trust that long-term memory.

After you've analyzed your data and asked students their opinion, it's time to sum it all up. Perhaps you have a mind like a steel trap and will remember exactly how you thought the project could be improved the next time you run it. But perhaps you will get caught up in the next rush of events in your classroom and school, and the details will get a little fuzzy. And when you dust off the project file next year, you'll find yourself saying, "Oh yeah, what was that major problem with the rubric again?"

To guard against this possibility, we've provided — guess what? — a handy form you can use to record your reflections on several aspects of your project.

✳ USE THIS TEACHER'S POST-PROJECT REVIEW FORM *(page 133)*

Collecting and Saving Examples of Student Work

Don't destroy the evidence!

Wait! Don't return all their work to students before you do one last thing. Although they might bring it home proudly or stash it in their locker until June, they're just as likely to trash it and you'll never be able to see it again. And don't you trash it yet either, much as you might need the space in your classroom, file drawer, or computer. You will find that keeping some examples of student work from your project is good idea. You don't need to save *all* student work — just key examples that illustrate what happened during the project, and examples of finished products that represent the range of quality you received.

Why It's a Good Idea to Save Samples of Student Work:

- When you do the project again, you can use samples of student work to show students what they're being asked to do. Good work can "raise the bar" and motivate students.

- Analyzing samples of high, medium, and low quality work will help you write or revise rubrics so they capture your expectations in clear, specific, descriptive language.

- You never know when someone may ask you to describe your project, and samples of student work tell a powerful story.

What Student Work Should Be Saved:

A record of the *how* the project was completed:

- Websites, books, organizations, community members, and other resources that proved useful

- Concept maps, research notes, interview logs

- Rough drafts, prototypes, lab notes

TIPS FROM THE CLASSROOM

Save to be Safe

Make photocopies, if you returned them to students, of all individual and group rubric evaluations or other notes on how you evaluated major products and performances. They may come in handy at grading time or for parent-teacher conferences in case of computer data loss.

A selection of culminating products and performances:

- Video recordings (with good audio quality!) of presentations, including the questions from the audience

- Copies of media produced: PowerPoint slides, video, multimedia, web pages, audio recordings

- Photographs of displays, exhibits, posters, models, works of art

- Copies of written products (electronic and/or paper)

After the Last Bell:
CLOSING THOUGHTS

Pondering Future Projects: the What, When, and If

We'll leave you with a few questions to ask yourself after your first project is over, as you consider the future of you and PBL. But wait a few days, maybe a week or two. Put a little distance between these decisions and whatever feelings you had at the end of the project. Find a quiet place and relax.

> Do you want to jump right back in and start another project soon, striking while the iron is hot? Or cool off for a while?

Questions About *What* a Future Project Might Be About:

- What other major topics in your course would be appropriate to teach with a project?

- What other 21st century skills do your students need to build? (To name a few: Information and media literacy? Cross-cultural skills? Ethics and social responsibility? Creativity and innovation? Systems thinking?)

- Are there some newly-emerging challenges facing your students and their families, school, community, state, nation, or world that students should or would be interested in exploring through a project?

- Did you choose the right type of content standards for the project, or could your students have learned the material just as well (and retained it for as long) if you had used some other teaching method? If so, are there other standards that might be a better fit with PBL?

Questions About *When* to Do Another Project

- Do you want to jump right back in and start another project soon, striking while the iron is hot? Or cool off for a while?

- Are your students excited about doing another project, or could they use a little time to relax with a textbook? Do you need to build some more of their skills before starting another project?

- How might another project fit into your course? Are there other units you know you'll want to teach that will not be project-based?

- How does your school calendar look? Is there time to plan and implement another project?

- If you'd like to work with colleagues, community members, or other organizations on your next project, when might they be ready and available?

Questions About *If* You Want to Do Another Project:

- Do you think it was worth the effort?

- Given the time it took, were you able to teach enough material to justify your use of PBL in a standards-based world?

- Did you enjoy the kind of teaching PBL requires? (Or did you want to go back to the lectern or a stack of worksheets?)

- Would you do another project if you could do it differently next time?

- Would you do another project if you had more time to plan, more help from colleagues, or more support from your school?

If you answered "yes" to the last set of questions above, congratulations! Welcome to the world of PBL. You may find that other volumes in the BIE *PBL Toolkit Series* will help you and your school go further on this journey.

If you answered "no" to the above questions, well, it was great that you tried, and we encourage you to try again at some other time, or in another course you teach, or with other students. Or maybe PBL is not for you, which is OK too — but pass this book on to a colleague!

Inspiring Last Words from Spotlight Project Teachers

Kristine Kurpiewski, *Product Comparison:*

One of the reasons I love to teach science is that it's "hands-on learning" for students. Doing small labs instead of a bigger project with the kids is fun, but it was hard to tell if they learned from the lab what I wanted them to learn — and making connections between labs was sometimes difficult.

Project-based learning takes out that guesswork and instead provides teachers and students with a framework for learning. There is a clear goal and projects often have kids learning more than one subject at a time. Because of the goal of the project, kids don't realize at first all the subjects they are covering in the one project. In my "Product Comparison" project kids learn how to:

- *measure and convert their measurements (math)*
- *make PowerPoint slides and use Excel to create graphs (technology)*
- *write a lab report (English/Language Arts)*
- *follow the scientific method (science)*
- *conduct research on ad campaigns (social science)*

My point is, there are so many cross-curricular components in a project, students soon realize that the subjects are not independent of one another and in fact everything is connected.

Anne Gloag, *Projectile Motion:*

I particularly like to see the applications of math to other sciences, to finance and everyday life. What I teach in the classroom is guided by what makes me excited and what makes my students excited. Students in my classes solve a lot of math problems that have applications in real life. Last year I also started teaching Chemistry…

students learn about big and current environmental issues and how chemistry can be used to understand these issues and how to come up with scientific solutions to our most pressing problems. PBL is so important in helping me do this.

Kristin Russo and Paul Koh, *Banned in America:*

Sometimes when you are in the midst of this work, you can forget just how truly powerful PBL is for teachers and students alike. Over time, our students come to internalize and truly own their education through these experiences. They always capture best why teaching in a PBL context is worth the time, energy, and commitment, like this graduate from June, 2008:

> Before I came to Envision Schools I never really cared about my work. I used to turn in my papers and just expect that I would get a decent grade… now I care about my work. I think about what I want it to say; what I want it to mean to people. By doing projects, I've been able to come to terms with who I am, and how I learn… and what I want out of my education.

The decision to embrace the rigors of PBL in your classroom or school community is a decision to embrace transformation. It asks us all (teachers and students) to consider relevance, to pursue excellence, to walk away from tallying the quantity of student work, and walk toward evaluating the quality of student performance.

What is most practical about PBL is that it asks us to embrace why we are doing what we are doing — and provides us with a 'reason for doing' in that all of the work is building toward something real, articulated and meaningful. It's not just the means to an end, because the means become the end, as the process is the content.

Over time, our students come to internalize and truly own their education through these experiences.

Donita Massing, *Design and Attract:*

As a career-technical instructor, I have used Project Based Learning every day of the school year in some capacity. I now look at PBL in a different way. [What my state calls] "Inquiry-based PBL" has changed the way I teach, and has greatly improved my students' passion for their subject. When students are given projects wherein they choose the questions that will guide their own learning, watch out! Be warned! You will get excellent results. Always keep in mind that PBL is centered around student inquiry and not teacher dictation.

Jennifer Ransier, *A Balancing Act*:

Teaching with PBL delivers a great impact on students. However, like any pedagogy, it must be done well. If all is researched, compiled and delivered successfully to students the in-depth comprehension of material is remarkable. It allows teachers to reach students of many learning styles and ability levels. In the 'real world' professionals are not given notes and tests to take and essays to write; they are asked to complete tasks. That is what a well written PBL project does. Students often express amazement in how learning becomes reality. I never hear the question, "When will I ever use this in life?" Students take control of their learning and strive to do their best, realizing that through a project, everyone will see their work.

David Ross, *American Archetypes*:

One of the most excitable students I ever taught was a young man I'll call Duncan. He was an inter-district transfer who escaped a failing school system in the next county. He had absolutely no experience with PBL but quickly became a convert. Duncan loved PBL. Projects unleashed a long-suppressed spirit of inquiry. Projects also gave him the freedom to open up socially, another suppressed trait. The minute one project would end, after I accepted his reflections and peer evaluations, Duncan would begin to send me emails. He would hang around my desk. The basic questions were always the same:

> *"What's the next project about?"*
>
> *"Who's in my group?"*
>
> *"When are you going to give it to us? Can we get started today?"*

Teachers new to PBL may scoff, thinking Duncan was just a hyperactive young man who enjoyed school. These teachers might think their kids will never respond to learning the way Duncan did. They would be wrong.

The Last Last Words, from the Buck Institute for Education

So, that's all for now folks. Good luck with your first project. Please let us know if you have any questions, suggestions, or stories to tell. Visit our websites, **www.bie.org** and **pbl-online.org**, to share with others, get new materials and ideas, and find additional resources.

Now get out there and teach those 21st century students well, with 21st century Project Based Learning!

USEFUL STUFF

This section has tools for planning and managing a project. (You can also download them from **www.bie.org**.)

- **Project Planning Forms:**
  - ▶ Project Overview
  - ▶ Project Teaching and Learning Guide
  - ▶ Project Calendar

- **Rubrics for 21st Century Skills:**
  - ▶ Collaboration
  - ▶ Presentation

- **Project Management Log: Group Tasks**

- **Project Work Report: Individual**

- **Project Work Report: Group**

- **Project Group Contract**

- **Presentation Day Checklist**

- **Project Presentation Audience Feedback form**

- **Student Self-Reflection on Project Work form**

- **Teacher's Post-Project Review form**

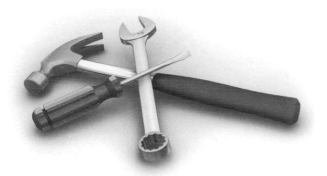

PROJECT OVERVIEW

Name of Project:		Duration:
Subject/Course:		Grade Level:
Other Subject Areas to Be Included:		

Project Idea
Summary of the challenge, investigation, scenario, problem, or issue:

Driving Question

Content and Skills Standards to be addressed:

	T+A	E		T+A	E
21st Century Skills to be explicitly *taught and assessed* (T+A) or *encouraged* (E) by project work, but not taught or assessed:	Collaboration ☐	☐	Other:	☐	☐
	Presentation ☐	☐		☐	☐
	Critical Thinking: ☐	☐		☐	☐

Culminating Products & Performances

Group:	**Presentation Audience:**
	☐ Class
	☐ School
	☐ Community
Individual:	☐ Experts
	☐ Web
	☐ Other: _____

PROJECT OVERVIEW

Entry Event to launch inquiry and engage students:

Assessments

Formative Assessments (During Project)

- ☐ Quizzes/Tests
- ☐ Journal/Learning Log
- ☐ Preliminary Plans/Outlines/Prototypes
- ☐ Rough Drafts
- ☐ Online Tests/Exams
- ☐ Practice Presentations
- ☐ Notes
- ☐ Checklists
- ☐ Concept Maps
- ☐ Other:

Summative Assessments (End of Project)

- ☐ Written Product(s), with rubric:
- ☐ Other Product(s) or Performance(s), with rubric:
- ☐ Oral Presentation, with rubric
- ☐ Peer Evaluation
- ☐ Multiple Choice/Short Answer Test
- ☐ Self-Evaluation
- ☐ Essay Test
- ☐ Other:

Resources Needed

On-site people, facilities:

Equipment:

Materials:

Community resources:

Reflection Methods (*check all that will be used*)

- ☐ Journal/Learning Log
- ☐ Whole-Class Discussion
- ☐ Survey
- ☐ Focus Group
- ☐ Fishbowl Discussion
- ☐ Other:

PROJECT TEACHING AND LEARNING GUIDE

Project:

Course/Semester:

Knowledge and Skills Needed by Students
to successfully complete culminating products and performances, and do well on summative assessments

Scaffolding / Materials / Lessons to be Provided
by the project teacher, other teachers, experts, mentors, community members

↑	
↑	
↑	
↑	
↑	
↑	
↑	

PROJECT CALENDAR

Project:

Start Date:

MONDAY   TUESDAY   WEDNESDAY   THURSDAY   FRIDAY

PROJECT WEEK ONE

PROJECT WEEK TWO

PROJECT WEEK THREE

COLLABORATION RUBRIC
(for secondary and upper elementary grades)

	Below Standard	Approaching Standard	At Standard	Above Standard
Responsibility for Oneself	▸ is not prepared and ready to work with the team ▸ does not do project tasks ▸ does not complete tasks on time ▸ does not use feedback from others to improve his/her work	▸ is sometimes prepared and ready to work with the team ▸ does some project tasks, but needs to be reminded ▸ competes some tasks on time ▸ sometimes uses feedback from others	▸ is prepared and ready to work with the team; is available for meetings and uses the team's commuication system ▸ does what he or she is supposed to do without having to be reminded ▸ completes tasks on time ▸ uses feedback from others to improve his or her work	*In addition to At Standard criteria:* ✛ does more than what he or she has to do ✛ asks for additional feedback to improve his or her work, beyond what everyone has been given
Helping the Team	▸ does not help the team solve problems; may cause problems ▸ does not share ideas with other team members ▸ does not give useful feedback to others ▸ does not offer to help others	▸ cooperates with the team but does not actively help it ▸ makes some effort to share ideas with the team ▸ sometimes gives useful feedback to others ▸ sometimes offers to help others	▸ helps the team solve problems, manage conflicts, and stay focused and organized ▸ shares ideas that help the team improve its work ▸ gives useful feedback (specific and supportive) to others so they can improve their work ▸ offers to help others do their work if they need it	*In addition to At Standard criteria:* ✛ steps in to help the team when another member is absent ✛ encourages others to share ideas, helps to make them clear, and connects them to the team's work ✛ notices if a team member does not understand something and takes action to help
Respect for Others	▸ does not pay attention to what teammates are talking about ▸ does not show respect for teammates (may interrupt, ignore ideas, hurt feelings)	▸ usually listens to teammates, but not always ▸ is polite and kind to teammates most of the time, but not always	▸ listens carefully to teammates ▸ is polite and kind to teammates	*In addition to At Standard criteria:* ✛ encourages the team to be respectful to each other ✛ recognizes everyone's strengths and encourages the team to use them

PRESENTATION RUBRIC
(for secondary and upper elementary grades)

	Below Standard	Approaching Standard	At Standard	Above Standard
Eye Contact & Physical Presence	▸ does not look at audience; reads notes or slides ▸ holds things in hands nervously or keeps hands in pockets ▸ posture does not show confidence; (fidgets, slouches) ▸ clothes are not appropriate for the occasion	▸ makes some eye contact, or scans the room quickly, but reads notes or slides most of the time ▸ uses a few gestures but they do not look natural, or keeps hands too still to look natural ▸ posture shows some confidence, with only a little fidgeting or nervous movement ▸ some attempt to wear appropriate clothing for the occasion	▸ keeps eye contact with audience most of the time; only reads notes or slides sometimes ▸ uses hands naturally, making some gestures ▸ confident posture ▸ clothes are appropriate for the occasion	*In addition to At Standard criteria:* ✦ keeps eye contact all the time, slowly scanning all of the audience; does not read notes or slides ✦ uses gestures smoothly, naturally to emphasize or illustrate points ✦ moves with purpose
Speaking	▸ mumbles or goes too fast or slow ▸ speaks too softly to be heard ▸ frequently uses "filler" words ("uh, um, so, and, like") ▸ pronounces several words incorrectly ▸ speaks in a style that is not appropriate for the occasion	▸ speaks clearly some of the time; sometimes too fast or slow ▸ speaks loudly enough for some of the audience to hear, but may speak in a monotone ▸ occasionally uses filler words ▸ pronounces a few words incorrectly ▸ speaks in a style that is appropriate for the occasion, most of the time	▸ speaks clearly; not too fast or slow ▸ speaks loudly enough for everyone to hear; changes tone to maintain interest ▸ rarely uses filler words ▸ pronounces words correctly ▸ speaks in a style that is appropriate for the occasion	*In addition to At Standard criteria:* ✦ adds variety to speaking style (lower or higher volume, change of pace, use of character voices) ✦ uses pauses for dramatic effect or to let ideas sink in
Organization	▸ does not meet requirements for what should be included in the presentation ▸ selects too much or too little information or the wrong kind of information ▸ gets ideas mixed up ▸ time is not used well; the whole presentation, or several parts of it, are too short or too long ▸ does not have an introduction and/or conclusion	▸ meets most requirements for what should be included in the presentation ▸ sometimes selects too much or too little information, or the wrong kind, about some topics ▸ some ideas are connected, but not all ▸ some parts feel too short or too long; too much or too little time is spent on one topic, slide, or idea ▸ has an introduction and conclusion, but they are not clear or interesting	▸ meets all requirements for what should be included in the presentation ▸ selects the right amount and kind of information to present ▸ states main idea & moves from one idea to the next clearly, in an order that makes sense ▸ time is well spent; no part feels too short or too long ▸ has a clear and interesting introduction and conclusion	*In addition to At Standard criteria:* ✦ has a memorable introduction and conclusion ✦ connects introduction and conclusion (returns to a story, theme, or metaphor) ✦ effectively uses humor, stories, or metaphors
Audio/Visual Aids	▸ does not use aids (pictures, drawings, objects, posters, maps, recordings, slides, other electronic media, etc.)	▸ uses aids but they do not add much to, and may distract from, the presentation ▸ aids are hard to read or hear, or are messy (writing or graphics are not neat or sound is not clear) ▸ aids are not ready to use and are not smoothly brought into the presentation	▸ aids add to the presentation ▸ aids are easy to see and/or hear, and are neat ▸ aids are ready to use and included smoothly into the presentation	*In addition to At Standard criteria:* ✦ aids are especially creative and/or powerful ✦ shows skill in creating aids and/or using technology ✦ smoothly handles problems with aids and technological glitches, if they occur
Response to Audience Questions	▸ does not address the audience's questions; says little or goes off the topic	▸ may answer some of the audience's questions, but not clearly and/or completely ▸ may try to answer a challenging question by faking it	▸ answers audience's questions clearly and completely ▸ when asked a question he or she does not know the answer to, says "I don't know" or explains how the answer could be found	*In addition to At Standard criteria:* ✦ answers questions in a way that adds details, examples, or new points to the presentation ✦ smoothly handles questions that are unclear, off the topic, distracting, or challenging

PROJECT MANAGEMENT LOG: **GROUP TASKS**

Project Name:

Members of Group:

Task	Who Is Responsible	Due Date	Status	Done
				☐
				☐
				☐
				☐
				☐
				☐
				☐
				☐
				☐
				☐
				☐
				☐

PROJECT WORK REPORT: INDIVIDUAL

Project Name:	
Student Name:	Date:

For the Time Period: Day(s): _____ Week: _____

During this time period I had the following goals for project work:	1	
	2	
	3	
	4	
	5	

During this time period I accomplished...	1	
	2	
	3	
	4	
	5	

My next steps are...	1	
	2	
	3	
	4	
	5	

My most important concerns, problems or questions are...	1	
	2	
	3	
	4	
	5	

PROJECT WORK REPORT: **GROUP**

Project Name:	

Members of Group:		Date:	

For the Time Period: Day(s): _____ Week: _____

During this time period we had the following goals for project work:	1	
	2	
	3	
	4	
	5	

During this time period we accomplished...	1	
	2	
	3	
	4	
	5	

Our next steps are...	1	
	2	
	3	
	4	
	5	

Our most important concerns, problems or questions are...	1	
	2	
	3	
	4	
	5	

PROJECT GROUP CONTRACT

Project Name:	
Members of Group:	

Our Agreement

- We all promise to listen to each other's ideas with respect.

- We all promise to do our assigned work to the best of our ability.

- We all promise to turn in our work on or before due dates.

- We all promise to ask for help if we need it.

- We all promise to share responsibility for our success and for our mistakes.

- We all promise to turn in work that is our own.

If someone in our group breaks one or more of our rules, the group has the right to call a meeting and ask the person to follow the rules. If the person still breaks one or more of our rules, we have the right to vote to fire that person.

Date: _____

Group member signatures:

_____   _____

_____   _____

_____

PRESENTATION DAY CHECKLIST

☐ Schedule of presentations set

☐ Guests/audience know when/where to attend

☐ Guest/audience materials duplicated

☐ Room arranged for presenters and audience

☐ Equipment / student materials in place

☐ Equipment tested (and tech support on stand-by)

☐ Teacher's materials in place

☐ Audience role explained

☐ Timekeeping device ready

PROJECT PRESENTATION AUDIENCE FEEDBACK

Group:	
Project Name:	**Date:**

Thank you for attending our project presentations and taking the time to write thoughtful answers to the following questions:

1. What did you learn from this presentation, or what did it make you think about?

2. What were the strengths of this presentation?

3. How might this presentation be improved?

4. Any other comments about this presentation?

SELF-REFLECTION ON PROJECT WORK

Think about what you did in this project, and how well the project went.
Write your comments in the right column.

Student Name:	
Project Name:	
Driving Question:	
List the major steps of the project:	
About Yourself:	
What is the most important thing you learned in this project:	
What do you wish you had spent more time on or done differently:	
What part of the project did you do your best work on:	
About the Project:	
What was the most enjoyable part of this project:	
What was the least enjoyable part of this project:	
How could your teacher(s) change this project to make it better next time:	

TEACHER'S POST-PROJECT REVIEW

| Project: | | Date | |

Project idea, design and implementation considerations	Reflections:
Student engagement	
Overall idea for the project	
Overall results for student learning	
Authenticity of project tasks and products	
Quality and use of Driving Question	
Scope: ▶ Length of time ▶ Complexity ▶ Number of subjects/ people/ organizations involved ▶ Use of technology	
Selection of content standards	

Selection of appropriate 21st century skills	
Selection of culminating products and performances	
Effectiveness of Entry Event	
Quality of rubrics	
Quantity and mix of scaffolding and learning activities	
Ability of students to work well in groups	
Ability of students to work well independently	
Ability of students to use inquiry skills and think deeply	
My management of the process, coaching of students, and providing of support	
Involvement of other adults	
Adequacy of resources	

Index

T

U